A Past Life Revealed

Mary Errington Evans

Truth through the Eyes of Spirit

A Past Life Revealed

The Wyndham Family
during the reign of Charles I

by

Mary Errington Evans

Regency Press (London & New York) Ltd.
Chaucer House, Chaucer Business Park,
Kemsing, Sevenoaks, Kent TN15 6PW

This book is dedicated to two very good friends,
Raymond and June Smith,
who were instrumental in bringing my husband and myself
together once more into this life.
Ray is a wonderful trance medium ably supported
by June, a most kind, caring individual.
They both operate the Gibraltar Psychic Research Centre
in Santa Margarita, Southern Spain.

ISBN 0 7212 0912 2

Printed and bound in Great Britain by
Buckland Press Ltd., Dover, Kent.

CONTENTS

LIST OF ILLUSTRATIONS

SOME THOUGHTS ON DEALING WITH THE WYNDHAMS

When I was first approached by Mary Evans to do the portraits for this book it was on the recommendation of another psychic artist, Coral Polge, and I don't think I knew what to expect. To be honest you never know whether a book will be published, so I suppose I was a little nonchalant about the whole thing and just accepted the work as I would any other request for a portrait of a guide – it would go on my list and I would produce the portrait when the inspiration came to me.

So, when the inspiration did come for the first picture, of Patrick Wyndham, I did not expect him to be such a demanding character. When we began to do the portrait I thought it would go as these things normally do and we would have a finished picture in about an hour or so. Not so. He would only let me work in short bursts of about thirty minutes and then, no matter how much I wanted to get on, I could not draw any more, he simply would not let me. I noticed also a distinct change in style with my drawing, as though another artist had been called in to help me. We had three or four sessions with him over a period of a few days before it was complete. So Patrick had made his mark and let me know that things were going to go his way.

I was then asked to produce a picture of Charles I and was somewhat apprehensive about this as I didn't want to be influenced by any preconceived ideas, but that isn't easy. I didn't know what Charles I looked like and if there was any knowledge about him it was buried deep in the recesses of my mind with most of the other stuff I half learned at school. So I began to produce his portrait and, after a preliminary sketch had been made, I was instructed to work in colour. Only then could I go and look up a portrait in the history section of a bookshelf. I was surprised by the likeness I had achieved, gave myself a pat on the back, and sent the picture off to Wales.

By this time, it was decreed that I was to produce two more portraits for the book, one of Thomas Wyndham, Patrick's brother, and the other of Malo, the guardian working with Mary and her other guides. Thomas turned out to be the shy one and was difficult to connect with, though we did manage but with me thinking I had drawn Malo. I was corrected by Mary, who was checking these portraits with one of her clairvoyant friends, since I am not clairvoyant and don't actually see the faces I draw, my hand being guided working from impressions. I was then left with Malo to sketch. Well I tried tuning in to him one day but couldn't get anything so decided to continue with some other work that was waiting to be sent off to a client in Italy, from where I had recently returned home.

Remembering the brief connection I'd had with Malo when we had produced Thomas's portrait, I knew that in his presence there was lots of light. I could almost see it as much as I could feel it. I asked if he wanted his picture in colour or black and white. The answer was a definite 'colour', with a reminder to show the light around him like an aura. Once we actually got started, the finished product appeared in no time at all and off it went to Wales, to be forwarded to John Thorpe, the manager of the publishers who have produced the book.

So it's been a good experience for me working with four very different characters, each working with me in differing ways to get what they wanted. And the publishers – Regency Press – were suggested by me as I know John Thorpe, after Mary's guides had already told her that I would put her in touch with a publisher who would take it on. Funny how they knew that, because you just can't say what material will be published and what won't. Still it's nice to know that spirit had confidence in their work, and so did Mary Evans. Somehow she just knew that what they were telling her was going to bear fruit.

I really do hope that this project bears all the fruit of its promise, because I know the hard work that I have put into communicating with spirit and producing the pictures. And that's only a fraction of the effort that Mary and her band of helpers have put into it. For me though, it has definitely been worth it for a whole load of reasons, one being the new experience of seeing one's work in print which I never really expected. And one should always seek out new experiences.

John Brett,
Psychic Artist.

IRENE'S PREFACE

My name is Irene Carruthers. I am a working medium serving Spiritualist churches throughout the country. I have worked steadfastly for 23 years with my lovely spirit friends. Mary and I have worked together combining our mediumship to write this book.

The experience of working in such close contact with spirit friends has given me such wonderment and enlightenment to know that my dear father from the 1600s, Patrick Wyndham, has given so much compassion and truth of a life revealed to us. Dear Mary and Penry were my grandparents in this life and time, in which we lived before. We are so very close, Mary, Penry and I; we have been to the very place where I, Anna, in that life lost my life with my dear mother, Margaret, by Patrick's twin brother, Thomas. He tried to stop this book being written. He desperately needed help and we held a spiritual circle to help him to come to terms with that he had done. He at this time was unwilling to progress to the light. Upon holding our circle, we did this by sending out prayers, our love and forgiveness for Thomas. We had friends who helped us in this task. As they sent out the power of love with us, Thomas made us aware of his presence, then overshadowed me and spoke to those holding this circle; everyone present told Thomas that we loved him and forgave him. There were two guardian angels in charge of these proceedings whose presence was felt with deep emotions by us all. They came for Thomas as he had now accepted that he must leave this earthbound condition and go with those watching angels to that higher side of life where he would find that enlightened world of spirit.

To be made aware of the Wyndham family, our past lives, the links and bonds formed with Charles I, have been a deep inspiration to me and will always be held dear in my heart. The friends who are numerous, including Charles, have through their dedicated communication given presence to this book being written.

Through our lives there is always an opportunity for each and every one of us to learn, for in history there are many gaps and conditions that we do not know about. We have been fortunate to be able to unveil a time in our history for this was the desire of Patrick Wyndham to tell the truth about that time. I hope for all that read the book you will enjoy the experience along with Mary, Penry and myself.

May God bless Patrick, Thomas, Charles and all those souls who made this book possible for without them we could not have compiled this truth to be told. We thank also those friends who have given their philosophy to encourage us and invoke within us thoughts about our world. With conditions, here we need to make so many important changes; Mr Shelley communicated this in his own philosophical poem. We thank him as this contribution most certainly brought forward the spirit world's concern for our world and mankind.

My deepest love and devotion to them all always.

Irene Carruthers

INTRODUCTION

I was brought into spiritualism in a most unusual way. I was virtually left alone after my first marriage had failed and I had to raise two daughters on my own. Life did not hold much meaning for me any more but I had always felt my father's presence around me since I was a child. I had also felt that there was much more to this life than living and eventually dying.

One winter's evening an old family friend suggested that I should try to receive communication from my father in the spirit world by means of using a ouija board that a family member had given me. I agreed reluctantly because they are very dangerous things to use and I would not recommend anyone to use one, but he persuaded me. We said the Lord's Prayer. I had no sooner placed my fingers on the message finder when it swiftly spelled out: 'This is your father and this is an elementary way of learning. I have a message for you. After I have spoken you must never use this board again.' He then began spelling out to me that I would hear bad news about a George. He continued to say: 'You must go down to Daulby Street Spiritualist Church, Liverpool, and I shall be waiting there for you, I have some very important information for you, please go.' He also instructed me to destroy the board because it took all their time to keep any undeveloped influences away from us.

The very next morning I was calling into my local shop when I felt someone tapping me on the shoulder. I turned around and it was my cousin's husband, Joe. He said, 'I have some bad news for you, Uncle George passed away last night.' I felt stunned at learning about my uncle's death. Nevertheless, it told me what I wanted to know and that is I had received a genuine communication from my dear father, Owen.

The next step was to visit the church that my father had mentioned to me. I arrived at the church and I sat quietly; I was then only twenty-eight years of age. I had never been to a spiritualist church before, I did not know what to expect. After we had sung a hymn and prayers were said, a lovely lady called Gladys Owen, who was the president at that time, introduced the medium, Miss Moran from Altrincham, Cheshire. I nearly fell off my chair with great surprise when she pointed towards me and declared to me that she had my father with her and he was anxious to communicate with me. The evidence she gave me from my father was astounding, even down to the Alsatian dog that had guarded my music shop, and other very personal details that no other person could have possibly known.

After the service, Miss Owen, the president, welcomed me and invited me to join the development circle run by the church on a Saturday evening, conducted by a wonderful medium called Bridie Tallon. A whole new world opened up for me and I felt I now had a purpose in life; my father told me many things through Bridie. One thing she told me was that I was going to be a healer, and, of course, my father was correct once more; I have been healing for thirty-two years and I belong to the National Federation of Spiritual Healers.

The president of Daulby Street Church, Gladys Owen, became very dear to me, taking me under her wing and teaching me so many wonderful things; she was greatly loved by all that visited the church. So I, Mary, have been most fortunate to be led to where I am now. I will always feel greatly indebted to my father, the rest of my helpers and friends who reside in the spirit world.

So dear Patrick had to wait until all this had taken place in my life. He decided to make his entrance when my husband Penry and I were having afternoon tea with Irene, on that lovely summer's day in July 1998.

I, Mary Errington Evans, was truly astounded when Lord Patrick Wyndham, made his entrance through my dear friend, Irene. When he explained to me the reason I had been chosen to write this book, you can imagine how I felt. Very humble indeed, these are the only words that come to mind. Also, the great surprise to find I was Lady Wyndham in the seventeenth century with two sons, Patrick and his twin brother, Thomas. Even more so that I had one daughter, Cloretta, and my husband, Penry, in this life, was my husband in that life, he being Lord Charles Wyndham.

I do feel it is a great honour and a privilege to be chosen to write the truth about the important events that took place in the seventeenth century. My knowledge of history was limited, especially of this time, but the help given by my unseen friends has broadened my knowledge considerably. The close co-operation with Patrick and the great love and compassion I feel emanating from him when we write has rekindled the love that I once had that had been wiped from my memory, when I was sent back to the earth plane. I feel happy and proud to have found that I was part of the Wyndham family, the love and respect between Patrick and me is truly wonderful. As Patrick has already explained the love link that is true never dies even after a few hundred years. In addition, as for dear Thomas, Patrick sends me news of him, because he is now coming to terms with his crimes, and is progressing nicely. I never fail to pray each night for both Patrick and Thomas. Irene, my dear friend, who was my granddaughter in that life, remains dear to my husband and me in this life; she is also an excellent medium. I am truly proud to be given the privilege of writing about part of our English history; although parts of it are very sad indeed, maybe we have learned lessons from it, who knows?

12

Chapter One

Wyndham and King Charles I

It all began when I, Patrick Wyndham, trespassed on the king's land in Weaverham in 1642. I took great pleasure walking those beautiful country lanes listening to the birds singing. I saw a lovely field most pleasant to the eye when I took it upon myself to venture on to that land. When some of the king's men approached and arrested me in the king's name, they immediately transported me to the king. When I explained to King Charles that I found his land most pleasant to walk upon and did not mean any harm, he graciously pardoned me; I was a young man with not a care in the world. I did not envisage what was to come from me being arrested on that fateful day on the king's land. There came to my ear a conspiracy to kill our king and I immediately sent word to him that his life was in danger.

His majesty immediately granted an audience to me and decided to accompany me to the place where I in great confidence knew that this conspirator was holding a meeting with other men intent on killing the king. On finding these men, I challenged the main one who conspired to kill the king. I drew my dagger, fought with him, and brought him to his knees; he surrendered to the pressure that I placed upon him. The others who conspired with him did flee into the night. The king summoned his guards and arrested this man who yielded up his name as Angus Larchwood. This dreadful scene took place in 1643 and this conspirator was transported to the dungeon; I took it upon myself to ask the king for leniency for him which was granted. I would visit Mr Larchwood in the king's dungeon although I knew that he had committed a crime by wishing to kill the king. As a loyal servant, I felt sadness in my heart for this poor wretch, who was to end his days incarcerated in the dark and extremely damp dungeon.

King Charles summoned me to come to the palace after this dreadful conspiracy had taken place. He then declared to me that it would be decreed by him, naming the king's honour to bestow on the Wyndham family and myself the lands that I walked upon on which I was arrested. In addition, he decreed that all the land thereof situated around and beyond the manor house of the Wyndhams be for ever ours with the king's blessing. As a thank you for saving the king's life, he also bestowed riches in money and gold; we served and honoured the king from that day.

His majesty entrusted me with overseeing the good citizens of Weaverham, which I carried out to the full. My main duty consisted of collecting land taxes and ensuring that the local inhabitants paid these taxes.

King Charles honoured the Wyndham family and we often visited the king. The queen was overbearing with his majesty and sometimes offered him the wrong advice, much to his peril.

There were many untruths said about me, as I have written before, but I prayed for my enemies for it made me very sad indeed to hear these untruths. I often reflected and felt sad when I thought of my king, that he had to watch his enemies most carefully. This of course restricted him from roaming freely on his beautiful lands.

The king had many enemies, though we would have our own spies in local taverns and coach houses. I would know of these spies who were paid handsomely if they uncovered a plot to kill the king. His majesty had to take care of his health as he was rather a frail man. He could easily take to his bed with some terrible illness, so we tried to protect him always.

His majesty was greatly misunderstood in many areas of his life; even the queen tried to overrule his decisions and so often gave ill advice to our poor troubled king.

King Charles did not want to be seen favouring the Wyndham family too much. There were those who, if they discovered the close bond that we had with the king, would have become quite troublesome indeed. Although my family and I helped his majesty in many areas of his life, we had to keep a low profile. His majesty was quite concerned that something could befall us because of our special friendship. Nothing could harm the great love and trust that existed between his majesty and the Wyndham family.

I remember with sadness the day King Charles sent for me when he was staying briefly in Oswestry. Moreover, I do not think he wanted to stay a moment longer than was necessary because Oswestry was more in favour of the puritans and so was one place where his life could be in danger. I found Charles depressed in many ways. He was running out of money to finance his army. Also Oliver Cromwell was gathering great strength. I, as a friend and one who would have most certainly laid his life down for his king, offered to try and help by selling personal things belonging to the Wyndham family, as did many other loyal subjects offer the same. However, the king seemed aggrieved by this and graciously declined my proposal; at least I was there to extend him a kindly word of encouragement to sustain and help him through this difficult time. He needed my company and to talk to me of his sadness over the constant battles and animosity from people whom he thought he could trust, and I advised him as a close confidant and friend, to the best of my ability.

14

He was concerned about what was transpiring in Scotland and Ireland. I think he felt trapped because too many things were going on around him all at once. He hardly had time to think and money problems became a major factor to him. He knew that his army needed to be equipped well and his men and horses had to be fed. Many a time his army and horses alike would be bogged down in the mud after heavy overnight rain and they would have to prepare to fight again that day. I visited many of the landed gentry and explained to them the plight of the king. They all collected items of jewellery, even cutlery and personal items, to sell for the coffers to help our cause. To relieve the king of financial worry, even the small contribution we made was greatly appreciated by his majesty. He was even busy trying to drum up support from abroad. My king had by decree given me lands so rich and fertile in appreciation of my saving his life, that now I took it upon myself to help him in return for his generosity. I received wonderful support from those citizens loyal to the crown; we so wanted Charles to lead us onward and to succeed in his endeavours.

I remember the time of the solstice, which you refer to as Christmas. I so looked forward to this time of year for King Charles would visit us. He would ride up, heavily guarded; he so looked forward to his visit with us as it gave him that precious time needed to be quiet and withdrawn into his thoughts. Yet I have seen him sitting rather unhappily and I questioned him on why he looked so sad on the day that all citizens were feeling jolly. His reply was that he was reflecting sadly thinking of the death of his father; I felt so sorry for him – Charles was a wonderful man. I know what has been recorded in your history books about Charles but I can verify that he was a kind and sensitive human being. He was a wonderful artist in his own right: he could bring out the most beautiful and sensitive colours I have ever seen. The paintings were enlightened with that special technique that he possessed; John Glen held some of Charles' paintings in the year of 1892 when they were very much sought after.

The Charles that I knew loved to be popular with people and he held many events. He would place two men at opposite ends and they would have to ride hard towards a pole containing a jester's head made of wood perched on top. The first rider to lean over his horse and pick up the jester's head to present to the king was the winner. Sometimes children's wooden toys were used and it all depended on the skill of the horseman to bend dangerously over to retrieve these toys, to great applause from the crowd and the king.

Charles took great delight in these events and he would sit and watch for many hours. Then, when he wanted to seek rest, I would summon one of his guards and we would help him to his bedchamber, where he would retire, tired but happy after the exciting day. The following day he would relax with a long pipe which we called a capor. Young lads at these events were given half a sovereign to look after the king's fine horses. Children on these occasions were given balls to play with because no doubt they would become bored easily with adult events. The balls were made especially for them out of papier-mache and coloured with very pretty silks; they enjoyed themselves and did not come to any harm. It was wonderful to see everyone looking so happy.

I was most fortunate to have met such wonderful people, in my time. I used to take great delight organising everything for the king's visit to make sure that his majesty would be most comfortable after his long journey. I would find stable lads honest and trustworthy to lead away the king's horses soon after he dismounted, so the horses would be taken to rest, watered, fed and groomed to a high standard. The lads would be paid handsomely for their labours. Even I took very few chances and I would choose to carry my sword, to add to the security of the king.

King Charles was always well received in the city of Chester. We had to ensure his safety at all times; he was very fond of Chester. Even to this day Chester is a very pretty place to visit; he loved to call at Chester on his way through Cheshire and North Wales. Of course, it was one of the most heavily guarded places in England and he felt safe.

He always wanted to be closer to his subjects; he often told me, his friend, his strong desire to be totally loved by his subjects. I know that he meant this with great sincerity; he was, as I have said before, misunderstood. He was much frailer in health than people thought and he often had to put on a brave face.

When Charles travelled, he often changed the route going back to Oxford as a precautionary measure because of the countless spies who would signal ahead that the king was on his way; and he thus stood a strong chance of being assassinated.

I remember the happy event that took place in Macclesfield; he stayed at the manor of two more trusted friends though he was still well guarded. Lord and Lady Hammersmith welcomed him and always understood when the king was tiring and needed a rest. The king, I may add, had a wonderful sense of humour but not many people knew this. People thought he had a dull boring personality, but this was not so. He was a wonderfully kind and sensitive man and it saddened me to have to wave goodbye to my dear friend.

I would often sit, on the very rare days of peace and quiet, and gaze about me. I would lapse into a dreamlike state imagining how, if I had the power, I would build up and transform my beloved Weaverham into an idyllic and peaceful place. Alas we lived in barbaric times.

I wished that situations could have been more open and free, whenever the king wished to see me, and he journeyed to Cheshire to discuss business matters. In most cases, he came heavily guarded but in disguise. I had to be extremely careful on numerous occasions for I did not want the puritans to find out about how loyal the Wyndham family really was to the king. I had to work hard at protecting him in any way I saw fit, though I would have gladly died for the king. Therefore, it became second nature to protect him; that is why the puritans decided to kill one of the Wellesleys, our neighbours, because no doubt the secret was out about our extreme loyalties to the king. Therefore, we posed a danger to them, when all we wanted to do was to live in peace.

16

When Charles was executed it was as though my world had fallen apart; a black cloud seemed to have descended upon me. When Oliver Cromwell had put his signature on Charles' death warrant, I am in no doubt that he believed it was God's will.

I lived with my family in the most troubled of times and yet the one and only thing, apart from my dear family, that spurred me on was the thought that one day we would have peace. Maybe I would walk our beautiful lands once more, listening with great delight to the birds singing; alas this was not to be.

I once had the opportunity to meet Oliver Cromwell. I found him a man with an overpowering personality. Also I found him a man of strong religious convictions and he was a strict disciplinarian with his own men. One had to admire his control; on some occasions, a compassionate side of him would emerge. I detected a steely look that would make a widow woman shake in her shoes.

Oliver Cromwell did not help matters, although he liked the king as a person. He helped to whip up fury in the House of Commons, when he felt that the king was overstepping the mark in certain areas of a delicate nature. This led to suspicions and untruths being spread about the king.

There were such atrocities in Weaverham. The king's enemies, the Roundheads, who were linked to Cromwell, carried out the most dreadful atrocities among our townspeople. I saw many of them taken to be hung or thrown into the dungeons and they spread untruths about the king. These Roundheads rode in with such ferocity and willpower – we lived in such barbaric times. Even people in our day called witches, who only practised in herbal medicines, were killed. Many of these unfortunate witches were gifted with having far sight into the future – what you would call today clairvoyant; they paid dearly with their lives for possessing these gifts.

Oliver Cromwell was not very fair with Catholics: for instance a lord was imprisoned even for making an unpopular remark about Cromwell or his soldiers. He would be made to forfeit his title and fined a substantial amount of money, often ruining him financially. Cromwell was not pleased if he thought the lord in question had been given the title and land by King Charles. It made him very angry.

Cromwell's army was very well disciplined when they were actually engaging in battle but, left to their own devices in the local community, they became bullies. Choosing to pounce on someone innocent going about his duties quietly, they would arrest him on a trumped up charge, putting the fear of God into innocent villagers. Some people relented and joined Cromwell after serving King Charles loyally for years. They were always afraid of very large fines, which forced some of them to sell their property. The easy way out for some of them was to swear allegiance to Cromwell and denounce what they had been before. Many titled people ended up in the most dreadful debt, because of this; even valuable paintings and things of sentimental value had to be sold. Having a title did not exempt you from serving in the most dreadful conditions in a debtors' prison, though if you had a few shillings left, you could afford a more comfortable corner in that prison with food thrown in.

Chapter Two

The Murders

My name is Patrick Wyndham. I was born on the 18th September, 1623. I was given the title of lord of the manor. My family obtained riches and land through King Charles I, decreed by him to our noble family.

My twin brother, Thomas Wyndham, was hanged at the Wheatsheaf tavern, in the village of Weaverham, Cheshire, for the murder of my dear wife, Margaret, and my beloved daughter, Anna, aged 11 years, which I shall speak to you about later.

All our troubles seemed to begin in the year 1646 when I married Margaret Wellesley, my childhood sweetheart. Ten months later my beloved daughter Anna was born to the joy of all except my brother Thomas. My dear wife Margaret loved to walk the pretty country lanes of Weaverham, with our daughter Anna. One day Anna decided to take a stroll down the track from the manor house to an open field that also belonged to the Wyndham family. She thought she would be safe. My brother had been in a dark foul mood for many days, brooding over the thought that my father would not bestow on him the title of a lord of the manor. This was to seal Margaret's destiny, along with Anna's. He stalked Anna, following her with light footsteps, so that the dear child could not hear him as she walked upon the land. Thomas pounced on Anna and suffocated her, then strangled her.

Margaret became increasingly restless at the thought of Anna not returning to the manor. So she went to search for her; she knew that Anna loved the land that they often walked on together. My dear wife retraced Anna's steps, only to find with horror our daughter's lifeless body. Thomas, who had been hiding in the undergrowth, also pounced on dear Margaret. He carried out the same crime of suffocating, then strangling my wife until she gave up the ghost.

When I discovered that Margaret and Anna had not returned to the manor. I felt my heart pounding with great anxiety and went to search for them. I walked down that pretty country lane calling to them, but they did not answer. At that point, my heart raced faster and faster with some inner knowledge that something dreadful had befallen them. As I entered the field and called their names, I narrowed my eyes to try to look further only to see two huddled shapes

Patrick Wyndham

20

lying on the ground. I ran to find my dear Margaret and beloved Anna dead on that spot. I placed Anna over my shoulder and walked back to the manor, about two miles as the crow flies.

We then returned for Margaret's body, with a horse and carriage accompanied by my coachman. I sank to my knees crying with such grief that I did not wish to live any more. Losing my beloved wife and daughter took a dreadful toll on my health. My dear mother, Lady Marriella Wyndham, was devastated by the two deaths and she drifted into mourning for many weeks. Thomas remained quiet but helpful to me upon my grief, not showing any sign of guilt or remorse, gloating in the knowledge that he had not been found out.

Chapter Three

Wheatsheaf Tavern – Ale House, Court and Gallows

The Wheatsheaf tavern then was famous for many hangings. The overseer of the tavern was a gentleman called Winston Brownley. He also held the keys to ensure that the tavern was made safe and locked by the end of the day's business. He was also appointed as a form of chancellor, or charterer, as we would say, over Weaverham.

My sister, who was called Cloretta, was married to a hard working gentleman called Sethsby; he helped us on the land as manager. My nephew, Damon, was a fine upstanding young man and quite handsome, may I say. He carried out the recording of trials and hangings that took place at the Wheatsheaf Tavern in Weaverham. In addition, he kept the books and he also recorded everything that took place, the only time he refused was when my brother Thomas was hung at that very same tavern. The tavern earned a reputation for the many hangings that took place there. He also recorded the taxes we collected from those farmers who owned land and paid those taxes due to the crown. Anyone who defaulted was instantly thrown into the dungeon; where they died eventually of disease or malnutrition.

Anyone found guilty of treason or any other serious crime was put to death by hanging: thus they would be strung up to the elm tree growing at the rear of the tavern. Then they would be cut down and thrown into the back room of the tavern, until the death cart arrived to collect the poor wretches.

Winston Brownley would oversee the hangings and conducted his job with pride, making sure that as quickly as the hangings took place he would ensure their collection.

Thomas often frequented the tavern to drink and gamble and he knew of a secret the tavern contained. This was that a holy order of monks frequented the underground tunnels, to pray and to hold long silences of discipline contained in their holy order. They also kept holy chalices and crosses well guarded by one of their brethren. On a particular day, Thomas noticed a man who had served in Cromwell's army disappear through the trap door underneath the tavern. He at once followed only to witness him, whose name was Jonas, draw a sword and kill the monk who guarded the holy chalices beneath the tavern. Jonas stole the chalices, after he had murdered the monk. Thomas made his presence known to Jonas and accused him of murder and theft, promising to report to the authorities what he had witnessed.

Jonas replied, 'I do not fear the authorities as my band of men, who have rebelled, see themselves as puritans. Did we not hide as rabbits in a burrow for two years until Cromwell came to power and then joined him, and even after his death we had an uprising to gain control once more. We shall kill those who try to oppose us; for Charles' nephew despised the king and joined our band to fight our cause to carry through for ever the puritan name.'

Before carrying out this threat, Thomas continued to drink the ale which the tavern provided. In his tormented state, he thought of the previous murders he committed. Then he started to ramble and to speak of the terrible deeds which he himself had carried out years before, only to be overheard by Jonas, who took it upon himself to report Thomas to the authorities.

Jonas went much further and reported Thomas also for the murder of the monk and the theft of the chalices as well as for the murders of Margaret and Anna. This sealed Thomas's fate.

Unknown to the Wyndham family, two days after the murder of the monk in 1672, Thomas had proposed to and married, in the chapel of St Mary in Weaverham, Lady Wynella Rivington. This happy union was to be shattered twenty-four hours later when five men entered the tavern and seized Thomas. They carried heavy objects they had collected along the way, and they started hitting him with great force.

These five men smashed Thomas's face until he was unrecognisable. Then they proceeded to smash his left arm and both legs. He attempted to fight them off, but pain overtook him and he began to pass out. When these five men realised what was happening to Thomas they dragged him upstairs and hanged him until the last breath had left his body.

Word was sent swiftly to the manor house of Thomas's hanging. With my coachman I travelled at great speed, whipping the horse to make it go faster. When we arrived, I collected my poor dear twin brother Thomas from the tavern. We travelled at great speed back to the manor house, with the poor broken body. I wondered why all these tragedies had beset such a family. Thomas, bless his soul, was buried in an unmarked grave set to one side to accommodate criminals of our time.

It was brought to light that one of the five men was called Jon. He looked up to Thomas and dreamed of being like Thomas one day. He was the son of one of Cromwell's generals, Jonathan Urquheart.

Jon Urquheart's family played an important part in Weaverham; his father was a powerful individual and was responsible for putting many people to death. Jon admired Thomas's stubborn and forceful ways, wanting total independence to do what he wished. Jon was a most unusual character with a dual personality and originating from what we referred to as the Dutchland people. He could appear most kind and accommodating and yet his underlying nature was to destroy those very people who had helped him. However, Jon's father did not like this friendship between Jon and Thomas. He deliberately ordered Jon to visit the tavern on that fateful day and to join in with the others to execute my brother. Little did he know that his father was behind the plot when the chalices were stolen from beneath the tavern and the monk brutally murdered.

This was a dreadful conspiracy and these five men murdered my brother. The cause of the attack was because they were all involved in the robbery beneath the tavern. We found out that the names of the five men were Jon, his father Jonathan Urquheart, Montellia, Denzil and Fredrick.

There was extreme envy existing from General Urquheart towards my lord-of-the-manor father, Charles Wyndham and all our family including the Wellesleys. The general had wanted to be a suitor to my mother Lady Mariella Livington but of course she won my father's heart instead. When my mother died in 1669, he felt free to extract vengeance on our families and he put a price on our heads unknown to us. Though we realised we were in danger, we did not know from whom. A breakaway faction of Cromwell's men re-grouped after the civil war, calling themselves puritans, continuing through to the 1680s. In truth they were a band of brigands, drunken louts and bullies, controlled by General Jonathan Urquheart, bringing more terror to Cheshire and beyond. To be fair, the true puritans were morally and spiritually good people. Everyone loyal to the crown at this time referred to their enemies as puritans for this description applied to any malicious and violent people.

Mr Wicks was the proprietor of the tavern in Weaverham: what a lovely gentleman he was! He was also a local councillor in the village; even the drunkards in the tavern had respect for him. He did not extract them with violence but, with a firm word in their ear and a steady hand on their shoulder, he cast them out gently. I remember the day when Thomas was murdered at the tavern, dear Mr Wicks wept uncontrollably at the sight of Thomas covered from head to foot in his own blood. He bent down and tried to wipe the blood from Thomas's face and the tears rolled down his face. 'Oh, Thomas,' he said, 'what have they done to you, my poor boy.'

Mr Wicks had known my brother and me since we were children; he used to observe us chasing each other, going into fits of laughter and he would chuckle to himself. I think these melancholy thoughts passed through his mind the day he tried to wipe the blood from Thomas's face, reflecting and hearing our laughter in the past. Mr Wicks knew what it was like to lose a loved one, for his lovely wife, Christiana, passed away at the age of 35 years.

She was a lovely lady and she loved to help people; she declined from working in the tavern so she went to work instead for Mr Brownley, the local miller whose grandfather was American. He married a splendid lady called Charlotte; she was also very pretty and a good mender. People would bring things for her to mend. Mr Wicks had a lovely daughter called Anna who helped him in the tavern. He kept a strict eye on the drunkards so they did not pester his daughter; he protected her and both father and daughter loved each other dearly. Mr Wicks, I may add, became somewhat of an expert at making barley bread and a wonderful barley wine; I shall take his word for it that the barley wine was excellent.

The barley grew quite well in these parts, but we also experienced bad times of drought. We would give thanks to God when the barley grew well. Mr Wicks loved and honoured the Wyndham family and we in turn respected and honoured this gentleman. Charlotte and Anna were a pure beacon of light to Weaverham. He was fair and just in his role as councillor and he had a very sympathetic nature so that even the local drunkards took great pleasure in being served by him.

In addition, it saddened me to see my family's graves without the family crest or names. This was simply because those in authority would not allow them because of Thomas's crime. So from that point I was closely watched. It was only by chance that I managed to rebury Thomas in the dead of night, when the puritans were too drunk in their beds to realise what I had done. At least I knew that I had done my very best under the circumstances. My friends who helped me put themselves at great risk for their own lives; if they had been found out I am in no doubt that they would have been hung. My dear friend who organised the reburial was Mark Manning, the other two were Isaac Bury, and Henry Woolton.

Even though Thomas had taken the lives of my wife and daughter, I could not bear to see them burying him after the hanging at the tavern in a grave set aside for common thieves and criminals of our time. All I could think about as they buried him was he was still my twin brother, part of me, who, in one moment of madness and jealousy, took away my family, because he wanted to be known as a lord of the manor instead of plain Thomas Wyndham. This title seemed to leave him deeply insecure and led him on to the road of destruction.

However I found myself weeping at his graveside and I vowed to have him reburied. This we carried out secretly with friends I could trust, we dug his body up and we reburied him with his dear family. Justice had been done.

Chapter Four

First Communication from Charles I

Charles the First took the opportunity of relaying a transcript to Irene, Mary and Penry through the trance mediumship of Irene. Charles spoke in a clear determined voice to Mary, who was writing down every word that he said. The date of this transcript was Sunday 13th December 1998. Firstly, he said that he was now in the world of spirit and that he would grace us with his presence for he said that he had important things to say that he wanted written in the book. He said that he loved to walk the grounds of Nottingham Hall, for it belonged to the crown and the land surrounding it. He said that Nottingham Hall served him well when he wandered in the grounds of this beautiful place. He also visited Oxford many times. He said that he had to be most careful while travelling by road, as it was most dangerous.

He said that he had had many dangers around him but that he made many journeys for peace. He went on, 'Judge me not harshly. I was twice poisoned and gashed with a sword; at one point a sword was actually put into me. Five men were responsible for this, then they gashed my shoulder with a sword leaving a gaping wound. These men were from within my own court whom I thought I could trust. Cromwell had them put to death. It is recorded in your history books that I had an impediment of speech but this only happened because I always managed to put my tongue in the wrong position. When speaking I told the truth. I worshipped my father. I was eighteen years of age when my dear mother passed to these realms. My mother's wish was to remain behind closed doors on her sick bed; she laid in a darkened, oak panelled room. With heavy drapes around the window, there was scarce a crack of daylight to be seen. I, Charles, grieved inwardly to see my own sweet dear mother lying so ill locked away from everyone except myself, her son. I grieved inwardly so deeply, upon my soul, I so honoured my mother and I thought she was most beautiful.

'I, Charles, would like to tell of Oliver Cromwell, the very same man who placed his name on my death warrant. He was a very clever man. He was likened to the fox in so many ways. For instance, he had a twin brother and one moment he would be seen on the field of battle with his army wounded and bloodied. Then, the next minute people would report that they had seen him with his army in a different location looking fit and well. This was a very clever man to dream up such a plot to be seen not to be defeated as such, but no matter. I, Charles, ruled with God's help – so many rules had to be adhered to but I ruled with my heart. Even a bishop turned his back on me – yet again one I thought I could trust. I could trust no one and this saddened and isolated me from those I should have been able to trust. The war that took place in my time was simply due to greed and dishonesty. Men in my time were men. I, Charles, was not effeminate as portrayed in your time.'

This is the second transcript taken 2nd February, 1999. Charles started by saying, 'I had to watch my back and those around me even in my own palace. One of my advisers, William Mollesley, took it upon himself to challenge my authority. He was also speaking at great lengths to palace officials and I found out he was, as you would call it, a spy in the camp. I usually had a deep insight that my enemies were around me.

'I decided to keep this gentleman as one of my advisers for a little while longer, because he was needed, but I did not trust him. This man was in his early thirties and I would say five foot eleven in height; he wore a long coat with a small hat with a brim. In addition, he always used the finest of silks in his tunics with frills around the sleeves; he never married or fathered any children to my knowledge.

'I had many advisers and William Mollesley was just one of them; the Mollesleys were linked to my family. The name at that time was very popular and used often.

'Marcus Mollesley, the nephew of William, went against the crown and joined up with the puritans. He was taken in as a boy soldier at the age of eighteen and a half years. He swiftly climbed the ranks and became a captain; he was, I may say, quite boyish looking. He often turned a blind eye to what the soldiers did, his face even became quite hardened. I heard that he experienced something quite unpleasant and this made him withdraw from the army at the age of twenty-three years. He seemed to age quite quickly after that. He was given the name Marcus by his Uncle William but this name was originally Marco.

'I would often sit and think most deeply about these events on the very rare quiet days at the palace. Marcus, I must tell you, managed to enter the grounds of the palace and he challenged me. I fought with him and managed to push him to the ground, pointing my sword to his chest. Still pointing my sword to his chest, I beckoned to him to stand up and angrily told him to leave. He left almost immediately with his head bowed. In my heart I did not wish to kill him, if I may be truthful, although he was an opponent of the king. This incident left me greatly saddened.

'Winston Mollesley was grandfather to Marcus, what you would call in your time a father figure. Winston was a great man and he helped several members of his own family; he was an uncle to William. Mollesley was a common name at that time.

'I have declared to dear Mary that it is high time that my beloved galleon was raised. I have used my influence and thoughts from this side of life to see that it be carried out. I felt so gallant on my ship, with such wonderment at the secret mysteries that the ocean must contain. The sea and the quietness offered me everything I so desired and never possessed in my life as Charles I. I always had to look about and be totally aware of who was around me.

'I did not go outside my boundaries or death would have awaited me. As you are well aware I had Scottish ancestors. I arrived on a visit to Scots Island; your history books I am afraid do not write the facts correctly. It was when I stepped ashore at this place I would be forced to make haste for they opened up with guns on us. There was a very large man who was unshaven with a bear like growth of a beard, which seemed to be matted and entangled. Even in my quiet moments at the palace I could still visualise quite clearly this man's face in front of me – the vision never left me. His name was Mr Tarleton. I went there to bring a settlement to the Scots but I am afraid I was not as brave as I should have been, your king is afraid to say. I truly felt that I should not have met with this man for my insight proved true and untruths were told behind my back.'

Charles then started to refer to the times that I, Mary, shared with him in that life, as Lady Marriella Livington Wyndham. He began by saying, 'My dear lady I have always loved you as a very dear and devoted friend. You always warned me and advised me on those quiet afternoons we spent together at the palace. You made the palace glow with the most wondrous light and I always thought you were most beautiful. People who worked at the palace were often afraid of you but only because you were outspoken at times but you told the truth always. I was always prepared to protect you with my sword.

'My dear lady, we spent many afternoons together. You graced me with your presence and I honour you in every aspect of my life. You were also well blessed with great insight and wisdom that you carry even in this life today. This book, my dear, must be written to enlighten the world. Please accept this beautiful red rose from me with my love – Charles.

'I have been given permission to tell you that there will be those who will visit your world and they will enlighten the souls of men. There will be some who will make their transition to our world without God's will.

'Man will learn in the future the source of the beginning of your world and has to overcome great difficulties. Your world has to change but there will be many changes in your world and you will witness many.

'I am only permitted to tell you a little but the religions of the world will not be the same for all time. I see more flying machines in your skies in the future and there will be visitations from visitors; mankind already knows some of this knowledge.'

In the third transcript from Charles I, he came through with this to say about history and especially of Charles II:

'It saddens me to come forth with this transcript, for your history books do not print the truth about Charles II and Henry, for we did not record all that took place in our time. History cannot record what we did not record ourselves.

'Charles II was born in 1630, the first of identical twin boys; the second was Henry who was not recorded and was taken by those who took our religion and knowledge, for safety and secrecy for a future possible reign.

'Charles was crowned in 1660 but was poisoned in 1664 by a Frenchman called Hoimoine Cartel. Henry took his twin brother's place secretly as the country and the crown would not have withstood the bloodshed which would have been caused if the poisoning had been made known, nor another coronation. Charles II was a very sensitive and gentle soul who fathered two sons. The first was called after himself and his father; the second was not named nor recorded. All this information was deliberately hidden.

'Henry became Charles. He was morally unstable but proved to be an excellent king for the country. In 1672 he changed his religion to Catholic but was forced to renounce it by a challenge from William of Orange, as the throne has to be held by a protestant king – which he tried to change but failed.

'In 1676, the French monks took it upon themselves, with French royal backing, to land on English shores, travelling from Ireland – as is recorded in a later chapter.'

Chapter Five

The Wyndham Family

As Patrick Wyndham, my family and I were very well respected in Weaverham. Moreover, my dear mother, Lady Mariella Wyndham, and my lord-of-the-manor father, Charles Wyndham, were loved so much by our loyal workers. They toiled on our land right through to harvest time when we rejoiced and they in turn with us.

My father and I were lords of the manor and, of course, everyone addressed Thomas as 'sir' out of respect for his position as the younger twin son of Charles Wyndham. However, we did not like to be thought of as aristocracy in that sense, we were only lords of the manor and not peerage. My dear mother, however, on her side of the family was a lady; because her family was of the peerage she was known as Lady Livington. When she married my father she was formally entitled to keep the name of Livington. I have mentioned before that Henry Foxton, the family lawyer, arranged for mother to sign an official document, giving her entitlement to use the name of Livington, so she became known as Lady Livington Wyndham. This helped in the sense that I often tried to drum up support from friends in the commons to help us win many causes dear to our hearts.

I cast my thoughts back to when there were happier times that we all shared at the manor. My dear parents were so devoted and happy, it was sheer delight to see them and they loved to take quiet walks together to discuss family matters.

Once I had the opportunity to visit Ireland by boat. My heart, I must confess, was lost at sea. If I may be honest, sailing into the great yonder gave me so much pleasure I can scarce contain my excitement at such a venture.

However, my heart was saddened to see so much poverty, though I loved these simple people of wonderful character on my visit to those shores. I exchanged with them small items I had brought from the manor, trinkets and pieces of jewellery, in exchange for pieces of wood carved eloquently and one item I prized above all – my flute, which I brought back to England.

I would sit in the manor house playing my beloved flute to our dear friends who would care to listen to the sweet sound of this delicate instrument. Oh, what lovely musical evenings we had!

I can still hear the giggles and laughter emanating from sweet little Anna, my daughter, filling every room in the manor, creating an echo. She took great delight in playing hide and seek with her devoted grandmother. My mother would take Anna to visit friends, to show her off like any proud grandmother would. My dear wife Margaret would sit with her arm around the child, listening to me playing my flute.

I loved to entertain in the manor house, my favourite guests being the Wellesleys. The house would ring with laughter, I would play my flute and our guests would dance merrily. We would exchange funny stories of experiences we had come across in our daily routines, meeting different people and situations that had arisen to make us chuckle, so to speak. My mother would read aloud to our guests the beautiful poetry she was so good at, setting down with great feeling and beauty. Oh, how it flowed! I could see that our guests were delighted and they would applaud. It was truly wonderful to relax after the worries and strains of the weeks gone by. So, after our guests had left us we were glad to retire to bed at least feeling happy that we had made our guests feel happy.

The Christmas solstice was one of our most peaceful times. I so loved to see the candles sparkling. I must admit, I really enjoyed the banqueting and the jollity and of course the feasting. It may surprise people to know that our jollity often lasted until dawn. Alas, we experienced a little bit of drunkenness, I am ashamed to say. It also brought me great delight to receive a gift – I think it brought out the little boy in me. I always felt melancholy and tearful on this occasion. When everyone had retired to bed, I would sit quietly and watch the shadows of the candles dancing merrily on the ceiling. Sometimes my eyelids would close through being drawn into the wondrous shapes of the flickering lights, and I would drift into a marvellously relaxed sleep, after a busy glorious day.

Christmas, I am glad to say, was a jolly time, a time for remembering and giving to those loyal servants who worked on our land, ploughing and harvesting for our sole benefit. We would have dear friends visit us, including the Wellesleys whom we looked on as family not just friends. Other friends would also be invited. The evening, after a hearty meal of pheasant and the delights of different fruits, consisted of playing at charades and singing the most merry of songs accompanied by my good self playing my flute.

We would rise early on the morrow and deliver food to those wonderful loyal workers who ploughed our lands and worked steadily in the knowledge that the Wyndhams appreciated their efforts in bringing about a good harvest. They and their families felt happy and secure in our employ.

My dear mother and father were a wonderful influence over me. They were so blissfully happy, content, very kind and understanding. The lovely manor house we lived in and the wealth we had did not change my parents. They were wonderful. Thomas was not as happy and seemed to find fault with everything, sometimes creating a scene. We did not know that the underlying problem then was jealousy and a feeling of deep insecurity, because he was the younger twin. This made my father very sad indeed as he could not change the fact that the first born must become the heir. Father remained sad until his death.

I wandered on our land decreed to us by royal command and my parents and I loved to walk by the millpond taking great delight in listening to the birds and the rippling of the water. If only such happiness could have lasted, for it was short lived, destroyed by the conspiracy within the Wheatsheaf tavern. With the beating and hanging of my brother, I would sit by candlelight and reflect on those happy times I so enjoyed with my parents. Little did I know that there were more unhappy times to come.

My thoughts often wander to my dear wife's friend, Shelley. Oh, what a beautiful lady and such a loyal friend she was to Margaret! When she heard the dreadful news of Margaret's death she fretted and pined for her dear friend. It was reported to me that this dear lady was refusing to eat upon awakening each day. Therefore, I took it upon myself to talk gently to persuade her to take in food, but even I did not succeed.

Shelley, Margaret's friend, was betrothed to a wonderful man but she lost all willpower and she never married this poor fellow. He was big and strong and worked our fields living to what we would consider old age at 60 years.

My mother was a source of great strength to me when my dear wife Margaret and Anna were murdered. Oh, how she loved her granddaughter! She would smile at Anna and gently take her by the hand and lead her outside and walk with her towards the mill pond, her eyes twinkling with love for this adorable child. After Margaret and Anna were found murdered, it was as if a candle had been snuffed out in mother's life. She mourned for many weeks scarcely looking out of her window. I was very much afraid that my mother's health would deteriorate quite quickly if she did not come out of mourning. Being the dear soul that she was, she also looked upon my grief and then started to pull through with great strength to support me. She would sit and talk to me and she would hold my hand and tell me in her great wisdom that the only way I could overcome my loss would be to throw myself into my work. She would support and help me. Experiencing such a great loss helped to motivate my dear mother and me to help those poor people who had also lost a dear one precious to them. We understood how one would feel losing such a dear one and trying so hard to come to terms with such a tragedy. Mother carried on with her good work, helping many less fortunate than ourselves.

My mother always put on a brave face when the puritan soldiers were around. On one particular day when they rode up to the manor house, she bade them good afternoon and invited them in so they could see that we had nothing to hide. She immediately told them to remove their hats, and insisted that they wipe their feet on entering the manor. Mother spoke to them in this manner to make them feel less important than they thought they were. It most certainly brought a smile to my lips, watching her talk to them as if they were naughty boys. The soldiers cunningly tried to get us to say something about some people we knew, to compromise them. My dear mother knew them for what they were and never would betray anyone to these barbarians.

I remember hearing mother let out a cry in one of the rooms in the manor. When I entered the room, I was confronted by a puritan soldier. He had somehow slipped through an open window, intent on stealing something; I confronted him and, luckily, he thought the better of his actions and fled through the main door. From that day on we were constantly on guard, making quite sure that all windows and doors were locked. I dread to think what would have befallen my mother if I had not heard her cries.

I remember quite clearly when mother was alive, she would invite on cold days some of the poor people of Weaverham to the manor house to partake of food and would present them with the odd rabbit or two. She was so kind. We tried very hard to portray being the lords of manor not too severely, may I say, as this used to frighten the poorer people of the community. Mother always found time to listen to them and advise them on different issues affecting their lives. I was so very proud and happy of the fact that these poor unfortunate people trusted us and felt the deepest respect for the Wyndham family.

My mother and I were travelling by coach to visit some friends in Berkshire when a highwayman, known in the area as Jack, sprang upon us and robbed us of items of jewellery. I had to shield my mother from this daredevil bent on causing the most anguish and distress to us, and one must obey when a muzzle loaded gun was held to our heads. We finally arrived at our friends' manor, distressed and angry. They were Lord and Lady De-Witt, who at once recognised the culprit when I described him. He was apparently making a very good living by robbing the rich. Jack was eventually trapped, arrested, and hanged for his crimes.

Chapter Six

The Wellesley Murders

The Wellesley Manor was adjacent to the Wyndham Manor; we loved this family so much and we shared so much laughter and love between both families. They would visit us and, in turn, we would visit them; my own dear wife was a Wellesley and I often thought how very fortunate I was to have married into this wonderful and caring family. Grandma Lucy would welcome us with open arms; she was a wonderful character. It was so convenient to have both manors adjacent to each other. If an emergency ensued then both families were in a strong position to help, in whatever way they could. This made one feel more secure.

After the puritans had murdered William Wellesley's mother, I so worried about my own dear mother's safety. I had a false panel in the reading room and for a few days we spent some time behind this panel. My fear was of the puritans arriving at the manor and I leave you in no doubt that they would have either murdered us or taken us as prisoners. We had arranged for a trusted friend to tap on the false panel to signal to us that the puritans were engaged elsewhere. After losing my wife and daughter, I was determined to see my mother live her life out to die a natural death, not at the hands of the puritan soldiers. I was determined to protect her to the very end. Thank God, she had a natural death and I was blessed to be by her side.

I would feel such sadness looking upon mother's face; she could never understand how people could conspire to harm each other the way they did. She vowed to help anyone who had suffered through these dreadful conspiracies. The rest of her days were filled with poor people who had suffered in one way or another at the hands of the puritans. Although we had riches and were privileged, there was never a dry eye in the manor house, whenever we heard that someone's poor husband had been dragged off to the square and hung.

My mother's kindness shone like a beacon, as a ray of hope to all those poor villagers. A dark cloud hovered over Weaverham the day she died. Cheshire was her home and she would have died to bring peace to the community.

I felt such sadness when my mother passed on due to heart failure in 1669, seven years after my father. Lady Marriella Livington Wyndham, my dear mother, was a source of great strength to me. She was a very well loved lady indeed, and she helped many people to come to terms when a loved one had died or been killed. I loved my mother with all my heart and, although she has now returned in a different body in this world, my love and admiration has continued into this life; my love for her has never died. Now, finally, we are able to write about the truth together and now we continue to love each other as if it were only yesterday, when in fact we are talking about a span of over three hundred years.

Mother loved the Wellesley family so much. When the news was broken to her of the Wellesley murder, she hastened to the manor to be with William Wellesley whose mother was so brutally killed in the grounds of her home. My mother stayed with the family to help in anyway she could. She appreciated the fact that Lady Wellesley had tried to protect the Wyndham family, but to no avail. The puritans made sure that this wonderful lady was not going to live.

Both our families had shared all this sadness and yet it helped to make us more determined and a lot stronger: they could kill our bodies but not our spirit.

My family and I held dear to our hearts the Wellesley family of that time. They lived on the neighbouring land adjacent to our Manor House. My dear wife Margaret was a Wellesley and that is how she and I met. We often had a musical evening and the Wellesleys would join us for a most pleasant evening of song.

The Wellesleys were a Quaker family but that did not deter the Wyndham family from becoming extremely close to this honourable family. We shared the most splendid of happy times with them, my own dear wife at that time was so happy it was a joy to see her so content.

I did everything I could to make our two families blissfully happy and, at that time, they frequented the Quaker church situated in Antrobus. The Wellesley family and the Wyndham family helped each other in all sorts of different ways. We shared everything with them and I often reflected on those happy family scenes to compensate for my sadness and unhappiness at the loss of my dear wife Margaret and daughter Anna.

I would help the Wellesleys with just about every aspect of their lives. We engaged a splendid lawyer, Henry Foxton, to act for both families. I admired this gentleman who was well read in all forms of litigation; this splendid fellow moved in more powerful circles. He climbed quite high up the legal ladder, to become most important in the legal world. I felt saddened when this clever gentleman moved on to goodness knows where, much to our disadvantage, should I say. Never were two families so close; we went through every form of sadness and extreme happiness together united as one large family.

I truly enjoyed those rare lazy days helping the Wellesleys on their land. I truly loved the outdoors, the breeze gently brushing against my face. The land was rich and beautiful. Although I was a lord of the manor, this did not deter me from working the plough. I would wake in the morning feeling happy and excited at the very thought of working the land, it was wonderful after a tiring day helping William. When we retired into the house for supper to partake of some rabbit or whatever had been prepared for us, we were tired but happy.

Alas, little did I know what was to befall the Wellesley family. William Wellesley was a wonderful gentleman and oh how he loved the wonderful big oxen that he drove on his land. I do remember the most pleasant of days when I would be passing by, and William never failed to raise his hand and wave to me most heartily. He was capable of speaking about the most wonderful philosophy: he was so learned and possessed an inner light of pure goodness. He had a great love of animals and I swear that his huge, powerful friend, the ox, had the capability of reading his master's thoughts. What a wonderful rapport they had together.

William Wellesley's mother had uncovered a plot to kill our family. One fateful day she was picking fruit in the grounds of her manor, when some puritan soldiers, who were the worse for ale, entered her grounds and cornered her when she decided to make haste. They grabbed hold of her and embarked in questioning this poor unfortunate lady, whereon they attempted to kill her. Not quite dead, she was carried by a member of her family to her bed where she died. Her friends came from near and far to attend her funeral, mostly ladies who honoured such a fine lady attending to bid her farewell, each carrying their own private and loving memories of this dear soul. She was interred at St Mary's Church, Weaverham.

William Wellesley had a sister who had a charming daughter called Claudetta with the face of an angel. We, the Wyndham family, so admired this lovely lady, slim, dark and pretty. King Charles I was instantly besotted with Claudetta, but unfortunately she spurned his advances. Instead she turned her attentions to a young man called Manson that meant in old English 'great one'.

Soon after I passed to the realms of light, I heard of the fate that befell the Wellesley family. It saddened me that such an honourable family should be wiped off the face of the earth.

In 1680 there came across the sea a man called Moembah of mixed race; never was a man so cruel. He joined up with the puritans and quickly became leader of a murdering band of louts who were constantly drunk and rebellious. This man was given money to hunt down anyone who was loyal in any way to the Wellesley family. Top of the list came Jon Wellesley. They searched cellars, barns, and people's homes; if they found any sentiments to the family in anyone's home the brigands would kill the whole family in cold blood.

Moembah was a very bad tempered, cruel individual; he even seemed unhappy with himself, taking great delight in inflicting pain and suffering on the most innocent of people who did not deserve it. He was a large man in stature, with a large head, an extremely wide nose with large nostrils and wide shoulders. I heard that, even if a lady should glance at him because of his strange looks, Moembah in a rage would set about the lady with a dagger.

Moreover, he would either slash her face or arm in such a way that it was hard to stem the flow of blood. This was to be a severe warning to anyone else who would dare to glance his way. This man, although he led this murdering band of puritans, did not believe in God and he did not have one ounce of compassion for his fellow man.

On one occasion he was searching a cellar with his men when they found a large casket filled with gold. It had belonged to King Charles I. He stole this gold and eventually, when he went back to his own shores, he took the gold with him on board ship. Moembah put every ounce of strength, tracking down the Wellesley family, searching endlessly, leaving nothing to chance. The Wellesley family had moved right into the countryside thinking they were quite safe; they had been invited to live with their cousin Jon in a large barn that he had converted to live in as a home. This murderous band came across the Wellesleys and Jon living peacefully and they descended upon them, killing the whole family, except Jon, whom they beat most cruelly thinking they had killed him for he lay so still. This cruel leader glanced around the room and, before he left with his men, he stole everything he could carry from their home. Jon lived but could not walk because of his terrible injuries. Some of the local people heard of the tragedy and they helped Jon to recover. He met a lovely lady who frequently came to help him and they married. They had three children – the eldest was called Mariket, which means to honour the king, another was Marikis, and the third was Welhem. Jon lived until the age of thirty-nine years. One thing for sure, this dreadful leader, Moembah, could not stop history being written and the truth told.

Transcript from Moembah

The man of mixed race called Moembah, the very same man who tracked down the Wellesley family and murdered them, took the opportunity to come through during a trance session through my friend Irene. My husband and I were present in our home. He spoke in a loud determined voice, halting now and then as though full of emotion and this is the transcript he relayed to us.

'I am Moembah! I have come to ask for your forgiveness. It has taken great courage for me to come forward.'

As he spoke, I, Mary, gently said to him, 'Moembah, you are welcome if you come with love in your heart.'

As I finished speaking, he replied, 'Thank you, dear lady. I am full of anger to think that I could have been so cruel in that time. I am now left for many hours with my own thoughts under the charge of the guardian who is ordained to teach me the right way. I left my land because of war among my people. When I was a young boy, I remember my father being extremely cruel; while my mother was with child, he did kill her with a panga or machete. He also attacked me and I was left for dead. Later my wife and two sons were burned alive in the war that ensued. I then left the country by boat.

'I wish you to know, lady, this was the reason why, when I reached your land, I was full of anger and hatred for everyone I came across. This caused me to vent my anger on innocent people. Now I have been shown the atrocities I committed, I wish to have the opportunity to put things right. I, Moembah, wish also to tell you that your own dear son, Thomas, is helping me to come to terms with my sadness and remorse. Thomas offered me his friendship of which I shall always be deeply grateful.'

My husband and I declared to Moembah that he would always be welcomed into our home as long as he wished first and foremost to go forward and progress, and to keep that love and compassion he had found in his heart. He departed with tears and a lighter heart.

Chapter Seven

Weaverham through my Eyes

In March 1642, the Parliamentarians took to plundering in Chester and the areas around; they had laid heavy taxes not only in the city but also in the countryside. They carried their wickedness even further by committing atrocities on the very old citizens, particularly men. They tied them behind carts and dragged them through filthy mud. Then these poor wretches were thrown into a dungeon and left to die which most of them did, because they were diseased from cold and malnutrition. May god bless these poor souls.

I often thought that I had been born into the fires of hell. My life held no peace, for I mourned my lovely friends, I held their friendship so dear to my heart.

I so desired to become friendly with the puritans simply to find out what they were planning, but I realised that this could prove quite dangerous to me. They had so many spies that one wrong move and they would have hung me. When I was a little younger I fought with one of the puritan soldiers; I sensed that he was following me and I took it upon myself to hide and waylay him. I took him by surprise, his purpose being to kill me. I got the better of him but decided to let him go. The soldier looked most surprised and fled. I often think that he found respect for me, because I could have quite easily taken his life if I so wished.

I so wanted to change the way people lived in Weaverham; I have seen some poor souls begging for a loaf of bread. Never have I seen such poverty on the outskirts of the village. I, as lord of manor, tried to help these people. Obstacles were placed in my pathway by the puritan spies, who said I was trying to gain a powerful influence over these poor unfortunate people of Weaverham which was not so. They spread untruths about me but my dearest wish was to help them through the winter with food and also farming implements, to help them till the land. It would have brought me great joy to see their faces, but this was shamefully prevented.

The Wyndham family was so very loyal to the crown and I was indeed proud of the work we carried out for our king. I loved my king and wished to honour him in every aspect of my life. His majesty knew that he could trust me, for I had proved this by saving his life. I felt so strongly that I could again lay down my life for my king if need be. Our family oversaw all the inhabitants of Weaverham to ensure that, apart from collecting taxes, law and order prevailed.

I was responsible for collecting taxes from our good citizens; one man who tried to discredit me was Isaac Weston, a cloth maker – if he could manage not to pay his taxes then he would. Some poor people could not afford to pay but this man could pay, for he paid a meagre wage to his ladies who worked the looms. I had to visit the man to demand the unpaid taxes only to be met with a barrage of insults.

He took it upon himself to speak in the square where villagers had gathered and there he tried to discredit my name saying I did not deserve the title of lord. Isaac Weston was jealous of the position I held as lord of the manor. He tried to give the villagers the impression that I never cared for them, which hurt me deeply. I was proud of the local people, and I cared so very much. At least I was respected in this field; I dealt with people fairly and allowed a little extra time, to give them the chance to find the money. It was extremely hard for these poor souls to pay taxes and they worked on the land from dawn to dusk. After paying taxes, I do not think there would be very much left to buy supplies needed for their families.

I was born into a life of privilege and I often felt guilty seeing so many people living in squalor, trying to manage on so little. At least it made me realise that I was in a strong position to try to help them in alleviating their suffering.

Two dear friends of mine were Jack and his wife; Jack worked the plough, often from dawn to dusk. One day he returned home after working hard on the land, looking forward to seeing his new born child, only to find his lovely wife had died during a difficult birth. I remember them with great love and sadness also.

I was under tremendous stress losing my dear friends to the puritans. My next two friends to die by the hands of the puritans were dear Jack and his son Daniel. These two lovely men were extremely poor and they lived just outside the village. Jack and Daniel were very fond of my family and respected the Wyndhams greatly. This reached the ears of the puritan spies at the tavern. They at once tried to persuade my friends to be disloyal to me and they wanted them to pass on information about our family. When these two dear friends refused they where shot. It does seem that tragedy seems to have befallen many of my loyal friends and family.

I was most fortunate to meet the Tsar of Russia, Nickoli we called him, and he was a most handsome and pleasant gentleman. I attended a grand ball given by the king to welcome the tsar. This ruler appeared to me to have the ability of deep insight not only of things around him but also of his own dear family.

Nickoli was a great man and a man of great integrity; I felt so small placed next to him. I was surging with excitement asking the tsar every question I could think of about the beautiful vast country of Russia. Oh how I envied him; there was a gentleness about him that I so admired. I referred to Nickoli as the tsar; I do so because in my eyes and in my heart he was the true tsar; even the people recognised that he should be the tsar.

Nickoli was a love child, ten months and five days older than Michael, because it was the father's choice that Michael should become tsar. Analyse was Nickoli's mother; she was quite young in age. Nickoli was not liked by his father as a boy until he became much older, when a deep attachment formed between father and son.

Weaverham had suffered badly at the hands of the puritans, when they had constantly raided the village. A gentleman called George Bromley had come to live in Weaverham with his wife, Anna, and his daughters, Sophia, Adiana and Christobell. This good man and his family became most helpful, supplying that which was badly needed. Christobell was most clever – she brought with her wheat, salts and herbs of every description. She put them to use by building up a store to which people could come and be taught to make a sort of bread that would help to bring a little nourishment to the poor people of Weaverham. Christobell was unmarried but she would have made someone a very good wife indeed, such knowledge she had attained, this lonely young lady.

We, the Wyndhams, loved our manor house and we were most fortunate to employ very good and loyal servants. In happier times we employed a jolly lady and her husband, Beth and Samuel: she cooked for us and her husband helped. He was extremely good at serving the food, and helping around the manor, keeping things in good order. We also employed a young girl called Mary. Her job was to beckon visitors into the main entrance of the manor. In addition, she would remove shawls from the ladies and coats from the men; to make them feel most welcome and comfortable, until I or another family member welcomed our guests. In addition, of course we employed a man who was our coachman called Jonathan. Local lads of course would come willingly to help to keep the stables clean and tidy. We had a main stable boy who was called Miele Watkins and he was very good with the horses, keeping them fed and groomed.

All these people were loyal and good to the Wyndhams, and we found them happy and content in these duties. One factor I do think is that because we treated them as we would like to be treated and respected ourselves; they were always justly rewarded for their efforts. Never would they dream of uttering a false word against us and particularly we trusted them never to pass on anything that they had heard in the confines of the manor to the puritan soldiers if they came by.

I loved to work steadfastly for the community but even I had to be most careful as I also had enemies. King Charles bestowed on me a ring, that contained the royal seal and I used this ring on important documents.

The king also acquired enemies and he constantly had to be extremely careful which often led to his majesty losing his temper, which was rather short at the best of times. In fairness to him, he showed great appreciation for that help I gave him, and there was a brotherly trust between us.

As I have said before, King Charles had many enemies, some in hidden opposition, who would use lies and deceit on the local population to further their aims. When I felt unrest among the local people who had been told untruths from these devious people, I took it upon myself to write sweet sentiments about the king on pieces of wood and I would place these on to trees for all to see.

Moreover, I would watch these people read with great interest these kindly words about his majesty, and I would observe them walking away in the deepest of thought. I knew that I had to try to win people's hearts over in the king's favour, for I told the truth.

My dear friend Jon was a recorder of all the lands around Weaverham. He trusted me and stepped forth to honour my name when he heard those talking who would wish to dishonour me. I was accused of all sorts of untruths that I over taxed some of our citizens when I was responsible for collecting taxes. My enemies tried all sorts of underhanded means to discredit my name, so I was indeed glad to have a loyal friend in Jon. It was also a sad day for all when Jon was killed by the puritans, purely because he was a dear friend of mine. They where a drunken rabble and they tried to make our lives most uncomfortable; these puritans did not portray any compassion or respect for our citizens, even the womenfolk suffered. They took great pleasure in dragging people off and hanging them, with little or no excuse and they seemed to enjoy the control they had over our people. As we chose not to conform to their wishes they burned our farms and cottages; this resulted in people being burnt alive. The people who survived lived poor and wretched lives. Our people wished to lead a pure and simple life to work the land to provide food for their families and to carry out their worship as they so desired.

I wish to tell you how we made the beautiful materials for our tunics and dresses, collecting various berries from the forest which we would crush to make a dye. Our women used special wooden looms and worked the silks and wool into intricate patterns; many women sat and especially embroidered the lapels, as you would now call them. The higher the position you obtained the more your coat would be decorated with very fine and beautiful embroidery. You would emerge as a very fine gentleman indeed, I myself did wear my corles (hat) for church on the Sabbath. Our women indeed worked hard and our much older and matronly ladies made beautiful lace to decorate the gentlemen's sleeves and cravats.

I undertook to manage with great care the lands that the king decreed to us. Many of our citizens were extremely poor and had to fight many diseases; some fell ill because of lack of nourishment; I tried my utmost to help these poor people. To live to the age of forty years was somewhat of a miracle in those days, which is why I helped many of them by employing them to work on the land.

My reward was not only by their hard work but by their loyalty also. Medical knowledge at that time was very limited indeed and I heard of physicians carrying out the oddest of treatments that often made the patient much worse.

I loved to work the land and it helped to bring our family closer to those lovely loyal souls who worked for us. I also helped the king with his lands to advise and help to yield a good harvest for his majesty. The king's lands I found to be breathtaking. When the king did not require me on a certain day I would walk on those heavenly lands, to my heart's content feeling the freedom and stillness, listening perhaps to the odd small rabbit scurrying along afraid of running into my pathway and the beautiful trees rustling in the gentle breeze; to me it felt as though I had finally arrived in heaven.

I remember those sombre times, when spies would warn us of impending visits from the puritans. Usually they would be drunk and in a disgruntled mood. This is where common sense usually did not prevail. They would take it upon themselves to spread untruths about people to use this as an excuse to ransack and search properties.

The Wyndham family took heed, knowing too well that these barbarians did not have respect even for titled families, especially if they had been drinking. We usually had to make sure the horses were hidden well out of sight, heavy drapes pulled across the windows, and doors had to be tightly bolted. This at least gave us a chance to escape if they became very hostile and our lives were in danger at any time.

A man called Mr Crossley provided Weaverham with much needed water, from his water mill. The locals would arrive with horse and cart and fill a barrel with water. Unfortunately, this man was not very honest and each time they tried to collect the water he would charge more. I, in my capacity of lord of manor, had to visit him on occasions to point out to him how dishonest he really was. This was not a very pleasant duty for me, as we often exchanged words of sheer anger, but these poor people were already heavily taxed and each day was a terrible struggle for them. Water was needed for bathing, cooking, and other domestic chores.

The puritans arrived one day at the manor house and helped themselves to our horses which may I say were splendidly tended by our stable boy, Michael. The puritans had lost some horses, which had been killed in a local skirmish. They would never ask if they could take our horses, they would simply take by force, if need be. It was a great deal safer to let them take what they wished; I was sad at losing our horses, for they had served us well, but the worst part was when they also took young Michael. They worked him hard, without taking care of his needs, or feeding him well. He was there solely to clean and feed the horses. Any complaints from him would have been severely dealt with, I doubt if he lived long.

We had no choice but to walk to our friends for the next few months until we were provided with another horse by loyal friends to help us out. In those days, we had dirt tracks and mostly fields, so it proved most difficult when they stole our horses.

I remember well that our family sold our silver and jewellery to help King Charles who was increasingly running short of money, trying to finance his armies and also his navy. In times of trouble, even the Irish army who arrived in Chester was issued orders to supply their own food, to take the burden off the crown. This army was grossly under fed anyway, but the king had to suffer long bouts of shortage of money.

I must say we did not favour helping the Irish because they were getting over friendly with France. The country at that time was quite powerful and we felt justified in feeling most apprehensive about this.

The puritans did much to undermine the good citizens of Weaverham by making false reports about them and attempting to confiscate properties. Many villagers were either killed or thrown into the dungeons to rot and die, if they so much as attempted to retaliate against the puritans.

The captain of the soldiers at that time did not attempt to discipline his men; they were allowed to roam freely to torment and maybe kill innocent people often in a drunken stupor. Captain Winston Mollesley took great delight in watching his men carrying out barbaric acts on a daily basis; even the old people did not get off lightly, being taunted and prodded to amuse those drunken soldiers.

At least we were lucky in that a volunteer would frequent the tavern each day as though partaking in drinking his ale. This spy, as I choose to call him, would listen to the conversation of the puritans closely to monitor when the next search and ransacking would take place. Then quite skilfully he would pass the word around to his fellow spies. They would also inform me and together we would plan to cover everything up that could be seized by them. We had to be vigilant at all times; never a day passed when we could allow ourselves to be complacent with our enemies.

Another colourful character of Weaverham was a French lady called Jocelyn Mandavey. She took on the dreadful habit of parading up and down the village street, trying to catch the eye of the men folk by raising her petticoat above her ankles, displaying a laced up booty and twirling a dainty foot. A gentleman arrived in our village wearing a hat and a very fine suit of clothes; he took great delight at the sight of Jocelyn Mandavey. Shortly afterwards they both disappeared from our midst never to be seen again; she was a very strange lady indeed.

I had to record whatever merchandise came into Weaverham from other towns. In those days we used to rely on large amounts of barley for it was one of the ingredients we used in our bread, hence the name barley bread. We also had to rely on the Welsh for wool, which came by road on horse and cart from North Wales; we used this in our clothing. A great deal of cattle rustling took place in those days and some of the sheep never reached Weaverham. We suspected that it was organised from the city of Chester, by the English not the Welsh. The sheep stealing was very well planned. They would steal the sheep coming by road with the Welsh shepherds in attendance who were too afraid to fight back seeing these English marauders stealing the sheep. Once the sheep arrived in Chester they were sold in the markets no doubt at a profit. It was very rare that the thieves were caught.

A man moved into the village called Jonas Derby; he was very good with sheep. He would walk many miles from the Welsh border with many sheep; he was what you would call a drover. Many times, we heard that he had to defend himself from sheep stealers but, being a large man in stature and very strong, he had the ability to fend them off and come out of it in one piece. Weaverham villagers liked the Welsh sheep, for the wool was excellent and easy to weave. Life was hard for these people; now in your lifetime, you have vehicles to transport livestock but in my day the journeys proved to be most hazardous; the men who worked with sheep faced many dangers travelling across country.

We had the honour bestowed on us of a wonderful gentleman who became governor, his name being Mr Fallowfield. He pursued a lovely lady, a Quaker, who wore a heavy brocade dress. At first, this lady, Judith Foxglove, spurned his advances, solely because she thought that she was small and dainty, therefore they would look quite odd together because Mr Fallowfield was very tall.

This wonderful gentleman did not tire of pursuing this lady and she finally relented agreeing to marry him and so becoming the first lady in the area. The wedding of this delightful couple brought all the villagers out to watch them; she strolled down the village street from the church ahead of Mr Fallowfield. She looked so happy and proud and it was so jolly to see the beautiful petals cascading around her dropping like snow at her dainty feet. All the people knew that she had married a most compassionate and spiritual man, who had helped many a poor soul, even many who had passed away. God bless his soul.

Judith Foxglove's parents called her after a flower as was common practice in the seventeenth century. This was our faith and belief; children are beautiful when they are born and they portray the freshness and the beauty of the flowers that surround us with so much delight and pleasure.

The favourite toy to play with was a wooden pole with a horse's head perched on the top; the local men would whittle these and made them to amuse the children.

Local ladies would make dolls stuffed with horse hair or bits of straw found in the local stables, with little tunic dresses. It did not take much to please the children because they were so very poor.

We had our odd selection of people in Weaverham. One was William Melton, a very refined gentleman but I always felt uncomfortable in his presence. He was most skilful at extracting information about people's private lives. He did not harm me in any way but he loved to add many yards to an innocent story that he had heard. This would seem quite harmless but we always had to be careful of puritan spies making something quite different out of what they may have heard.

He forcibly invited himself to the manor house and, when he arrived, he wanted me to take him on a tour of the house, which I declined saying that he would disturb other people residing in the house. I chuckled when this odd gentleman left my presence.

Because of our influence as lords of the manor, we were in a position to help people like one, William Mollesley, who wished to meet the appropriate people to gain a licence to import wheat from the colonies. He being of good character, I agreed to help him with this so I arranged for him to meet the people that dealt with imports and exports in the lucrative shipping section. I would never help people in this sense to gain reward in any way whatsoever. I knew that by helping people like this gentleman, it had a dramatic effect on helping our towns and villages, which badly needed the business. I also felt that exchanging food or cloth with different countries would help to stabilise relations between countries who traded with us.

Samual Whinney was a most interesting person; he was the local undertaker and the only one that Weaverham had. He was a very busy man travelling backwards and forwards to the tavern collecting the bodies of the poor souls who had been hung. The boxes or coffins were of a very crude nature. The poor relatives tried to honour these poor wretches with a decent funeral and would collect a few wild flowers to place on the grave. Samual Whinney would state with great conviction that he was far too busy collecting the dear departed to be able to utter a prayer over the poor soul's coffin. Therefore, he would leave this delicate task to the relatives and to the person who officiated at the graveside.

I looked forward to attending church, or 'capel' as we referred to it on occasions; I would wear my corles (hat) on that special day. One had to have a very good excuse to miss the very early morning service on the Sabbath. The minister, the Revd William Wentworth, was very strict and expected the children to walk into church in an orderly fashion. The children were not allowed to utter one word, unless spoken to. It was a day of great discipline and commitment to God. On entering, the men would raise their hats out of respect to the minister and to the ladies attending. The ladies were expected to dress soberly in browns or greys; they were not allowed to dress brightly, nor were they allowed to glance at gentlemen. Neither were the gentlemen in turn to glance at the ladies. I must say it taught one great discipline.

The Wyndham family lawyer was Henry Foxton, a very clever man indeed, but Weaverham had its own lawyer, Michael Morrisey. This gentleman was consulted by the local people on litigation concerning land and boundaries, where many quarrels took place, particularly if someone's sheep trespassed on another man's land, where perhaps the boundary had not been secured properly. Michael Morrisey was a very strong character and he had the ability to put the fear of God into people if they refused to back down on a legal issue. He knew Henry Foxton, but I must say that he never became such a fine lawyer. Henry Foxton travelled further afield to Norfolk and made an honourable name for himself in the legal establishment but I do think that Michael Morrisey was quite content quelling the discontented people of Weaverham.

Antrobus was a pretty little village not far from Weaverham; there was only one thing that spoiled the serenity and peace. We Wyndhams often visited this lovely place to see my dear friend Mr Wellington, who possessed a lovely little dog called Brutus. This little dog would greet us with friendly little yaps and funny little noises to let us know that he was glad to see us. All this friendliness and happiness was spoilt by having to watch our backs, for the puritans had a stranglehold on the place. With spies strategically placed one could speak quite openly to a friend, only to find out a few days later that the friend that you had visited had been arrested and questioned in a dreadful and cruel way. I always had to be so careful.

I remember an incident that took place at the tavern in Weaverham. The memory of Thomas came flooding back to me and it caused me pain. Puritan soldiers savagely killed the man known to us as Michael Mollesley, who helped us tend the gardens and grounds of the manor house. He was overheard to criticise the puritans, saying that they should leave the people of Weaverham in peace. A few days later, while visiting the tavern, once more some puritan soldiers arrested him but, instead of taking him to the dungeon, they tied him behind a horse and cart and dragged him to his death through the village, to the horror of the village people. I found I could not sleep that night for it brought back that dreadful nightmare of collecting my brother's broken body, after the puritans had killed him.

Life was extremely hard for those poorer women who lived in the village. Nell and Tom Maudesley had the task of taking care of the young children of the women who worked in the fields. Once a woman had reached the age of thirty she was considered too old to work in the fields. Life expectancy of a woman was thirty-five years of age in the 17th century; this age was considered quite old. Among the poorer community, these people ate a large amount of rye bread; this bread was recognised as the food of the poorer classes. These people were ill quite frequently because of the poor diet and of course the worry of trying to feed their families particularly in the harsh winter months.

A family of cloth makers moved into Weaverham called Menlove bringing badly needed employment to Weaverham in 1667. They dyed the cloth, which was transported by horse and cart to London to clothe the rich people, the gentry. They were extremely good cloth makers but, unfortunately, the poor people could not afford to clothe themselves in this cloth, only to admire the finished garment on the very rich wearer. Swords and nails were made in Birmingham at that time, while Chester was well documented for making shoes and gloves, and a person was not properly dressed unless they finished off their

King Charles I

attire with gloves. The more lace a gentleman wore on his sleeve told that he was not short of a penny or two.

I was quite saddened at times to witness some of our people on the run, terrified that the puritans would catch them. The Wyndhams would often hide these poor souls, they being just ordinary farming people and those trying to make a meagre living out of trading between each other, selling barley bread, fruits and an assortment of different things, struggling to scratch a living.

We, the Wyndham family, tried to help by hiding these poor wretches in barns on our land and covering them over with straw. At a given time when we knew that the puritans had gone we signalled to them to come out but we also managed to leave them some food to strengthen them for their onward journey to goodness knows where.

A gentleman who was very well respected in Weaverham was a physician by the name of Mr Ormend. He was recognised by the villagers by the extremely long coat that he wore. He was always kept busy; we would observe him riding swiftly by on his fiery stallion delivering medicine to the sick. What a glorious sight we did see, Mr Ormend riding by followed quickly by his lovely faithful companion, Sable, who was a spaniel dog. If the stallion sped off at great speed, you could be sure the little dog would not be far behind panting and enjoying keeping up this great pace with the horse. Sable was rescued off the streets by the doctor and he would draw the dear little dog to his chest and hug him, as though he were a dear lost friend that he had just found. He so enjoyed this lovely animal's companionship and I knew that Sable felt the same way about Mr Ormend.

Sethsby Wells was the local blacksmith; he was a large strong gentleman, quite capable of lifting three saddles in one lift without drawing his breath. He was also a strong individual in the sense that he was afraid of no one. He was not afraid of the puritans, even though they used him for many tasks outside his trade. He had a lovely wife called Mary and three children; he often volunteered to help us on our land during harvesting. I would gaze at this man in sheer amazement of his strength. Often I wished that I was as strong as this likeable man was; he was quick in thought and could turn his hand to just about anything. He was extremely clever I thought. The villagers seemed to like Sethsby and I think that, because of his size, they somehow felt protected by him. In those days not many people were tall.

I was instrumental in bringing about a fairer trial system at the tavern. If a certain individual was known to be guilty, then whoever was overseeing at the time would automatically sign a document and the poor man would be either hung or for a lesser offence thrown into the local dungeon. I took it upon myself to visit King Charles to speak with him on this delicate matter of people being given the right to a fair trial. There were far too many lynchings without these poor souls being represented in some way to prove their innocence. It took a great deal of time and effort. I consulted with a Mr Pym and as many influential people that I could in the House of Commons to try to sway them to see my point of view. Eventually I received the king's blessing. He spoke about the matter to those in the judiciary and he helped to bring in a more humane system.

If you were very poor in the 17th century you could plead for your life from dawn to dusk but it would be ignored, I am afraid. Even if your family was to starve, this simply did not matter. I simply could not live with my conscience any longer and I felt the time was right. I think that the king understood fully how I felt about this barbaric injustice, for he saw my point of view. In addition, I feel that the determined look on my face said it all perfectly.

I always tried to influence those people who employed the local villagers, for these poor villagers were on such poor wages that they were reaching extreme poverty. In addition, worst of all should they succumb to temptation and were caught, they could spend the remainder of their lives in the dungeon, even for stealing a loaf of barley bread. I succeeded in persuading some employers to pay a little more to these poor wretches. Like Mr Livingstone, a saddler I found to my amazement that he supported me in my efforts to bring about better conditions for them even with a few pence more. Those employers who could not afford to pay any more, I managed to persuade to pay in kind with much needed food like rabbit and fruit and whatever they could offer to sustain their workers. I felt well pleased.

Children in those days were not thought to be important enough to worry about. We Wyndhams offered financial help to educate these children and I spoke at great length to a Mr Neville Morris, who thought of himself as very powerful and most important in the community. I am afraid he was not willing to listen or to try and make life a little easier for these poor unfortunate children. We so loved children and to see them suffer in such a way, used to bring tears to my eyes. To be born terribly poor was bad enough, so sickly that you did not have the strength to stand up straight, not a week went by when we did not witness the death of one of our children.

The farming community took great pride in their work and I often rode around the small farmsteads to advise and encourage those farming people who may have experienced a bad harvest. I did so love the land, I took it upon myself to visit these people and, if it were within my power, I would help them. I do remember some very bad harvests because of very bad weather. I can remember quite clearly the snow above the hedgerows, it was a pretty sight but not very pleasant to try to walk in. Moreover, it was pitiful to see those poor villagers with threadbare clothing on, when it was snowing so hard that one's face and hands did hurt so. The gentleman I appointed to make my tunics was called Mr Sykes, and he did dwell in Weaverham. Cloth then was of very poor quality, and it was quite difficult for him to keep stocks of cloth because the army needed most of it to make uniforms and they had first choice. That left very little for us. Most of our wool was obtained from Norfolk and Wales. He was a jolly sort of man and he was quite gifted at making very fine tunics indeed. Most of the poor people had to make do with rough sackcloth, which was also quite unattractive and reddened the skin of the wearer. The picture you see of me is in one of those tunics, wine coloured edged around the collar in gold thread, what you would call in your time your best suit.

Religion has been the cause of many wars and the 17th century was no exception. I remember the day when the villagers of Weaverham took up arms against a purge on the village by puritan soldiers. They blatantly entered homes of known Catholic villagers and went into each room looking for any signs of crucifixes on the walls. When the poor citizens of Weaverham tried to stop them they were dragged from their homes and beaten. Anyone who fought back vigorously were dragged off to the dungeon, never to be seen again. The villagers fought with anything that was on hand but the soldiers got the better of them. They of course were usually the worse for drink and so they were in an ugly mood. It was sad to see ordinary hard working people, treated with such disrespect.

We had some very good souls in Weaverham and one family stood out to be applauded: they were Winston and Molly who were husband and wife and Protestant. Many of our villagers who were dragged from their homes and beaten managed to slip away from the soldiers. After dark, this couple took the poor people into their home, bathed and soothed their wounds and tended to their needs. They being Protestant could have quite easily made a small fortune acting as spies. People would also be in trouble for just bowing to a cross. But the dear people whom I call spiritual would not even contemplate such a thing. They of course put their own lives at risk by just being compassionate and caring.

The dungeons in the 17th century would make one shudder. I remember visiting Angus Larchwood, the man who tried to kill the king. The sight that met my eyes was dreadful: the only window within the confines of the dungeon was so high up the sun scarcely came in; stinking water dripped down the walls leaving puddles; and one could hear the rats scurrying to and fro squealing in unison. I felt so sorry for that poor man; he was very slight of build with auburn hair. I felt that this place most certainly must be based on one's imagination of what hell must look like.

I think that is why I became stronger after the deaths of Margaret and Anna. I felt so much compassion on hearing tales of those poor people who had been incarcerated but who had been lucky enough to serve their sentence and set free.

Nevertheless, it was quite rare for anyone to survive those harsh conditions, and yet some did. They must have possessed a very strong will to live.

I often tried to speak out about these dreadful conditions but all the judiciary would say was that places like that were justified and likened the poor prisoners to rats in ships. Some of the crimes were quite petty but people would still find themselves being thrown into the dungeon, even for the theft of a loaf of bread, even for speaking about the puritans in a nasty way. Ordinary citizens were not allowed to have freedom of speech: this was determined as treachery. If a lord served time as a prisoner in the dungeon, he was allowed to buy his way out or have some of his land confiscated.

I remember my family and I decided to take advantage of a lovely evening and we travelled by coach and horse to visit friends a few miles away. On returning we found puritan soldiers waiting for us outside the manor house. They wanted to search the house to see if we had been harbouring a Roman Catholic on the run from the puritans. After we entered the manor we let the soldiers search the house from top to bottom. If by chance they had found someone hiding, that would have been punished with death by hanging. Sometimes we did hide people but this time we were lucky for they found nothing.

In the 17th century, we had debtors' prisons. If a person was unable to pay his debts then automatically he would be placed in the prison. If the family could not afford to take food into that person in prison, then the poor unfortunate would die of starvation. Sometimes if one of our villagers had cause to be called to the tavern to answer a debtor's charge, I would volunteer to help him or her to pay the debt, thus avoiding being thrown into the debtors' prison. If however they could not honour the debt and pay me the sum of money back, then I would require them to help on the Wyndham estate, as long as they were fit and able. They were always glad to co-operate with this arrangement as it left them free to be with their families.

We in Weaverham had another surprise to come. There arrived in 1672 settlers from what we then used to call the Dutchlands. They brought with them such strictness and realism to the village of Weaverham. They knew the workings of the land but we were in great suspicion of them as they seemed secretive and did not engage in too much conversation.

I remember with great fondness a lovely lady called Mariana, who had beautiful long dark hair; she wore a long dress and over it an apron. She worked in the tavern where poor Thomas was hung. Her father, Wilhelm, was from the Dutchlands and he had tuberculosis. He was a small man and could not work because he was so ill; he even suffered greatly with pains in his hands. The tavern was a busy place because people used to travel from other towns as Weaverham was such a pretty village, and still is. Poor Mariana never married although many a man pushed himself forward boldly. She devoted herself to taking care and nursing her very sick father.

We had a local bookkeeper of sorts in Weaverham; Joshua Swain kept the books and audited all the goods coming into Weaverham. He was responsible for safely storing such goods. Dyed cloth was stored, among other things, in readiness to be shipped to London or taken by horse and cart to other towns. Of course wool was kept in readiness for the spinners. Some women worked from home spinning; everyone had an important job to do to keep Weaverham going. Wages in the 17th century were extremely poor and the spinners were kept busy every day.

We Wyndhams were for ever on our guard. One such day comes to mind when we heard of the plight of Mr Jacobs who owned a smallholding in Weaverham. Unfortunately, while drinking in the Wheatsheaf tavern he was overheard by a spy to shout and curse Oliver Cromwell's name, saying that this evil man should lose his head. Shortly after leaving the tavern, the puritan soldiers arrived at his smallholding and set it alight, hoping to burn this poor unfortunate man alive. Luckily Mr Jacobs had stopped by to deliver a jug of ale to one of his neighbours who hid him swiftly until the soldiers had departed. On hearing about this man's plight, we secretly arranged to have him sent in safety to another town. There is no doubt if he had stayed his fate would have been the dungeon or dragged to the square to be hung. He lost many sentimental possessions including livestock but it was most unwise to stay. One could never feel safe; it was very hard indeed not to keep to oneself the bitterness welling up inside. This often exploded with some people particularly those who had seen atrocities at the hands of the puritans and had lost friends and family. There were no such luxuries as free speech in the 17th century like most people enjoy in your world today.

Mr Naseby was a very fine gentleman. He lived on the outskirts of the village in a reasonably large house of that time. He was known as a country squire. He was a well-educated man and he lived with his widowed sister, Emily, plus a housekeeper. He also had a lovely little dog called Spot because of a white spot at the side of the little dog's head. Spot was a lovely brown colour and this little fellow was so well behaved. When Mr Naseby pointed his fancy stick towards the dog, the little creature would immediately sit and look up quite lovingly to his master. This gentleman whenever he travelled into the village would offer his services free of charge to anyone illiterate who needed help or advice. He felt saddened at the fact that many of the people could not read or write and were totally uneducated.

We at least had many kind people in Weaverham and this helped to offset any miseries that we had to endure. I was very fortunate to have had a good education but for this to take place one would have to possess money to carry on with one's studies both academic and musical. People in our time led wretched lives if they did not have the ability to read or write, and often they would be ridiculed by harsh employers even if they carried out the simplest of jobs. I was most grateful to be privileged with having such a good education, and in turn to help my sister's boy, Damon, to receive a good education to enable him to carry out the important work set down for him to do as recorder to the tavern.

Molly Jennings and her husband Jack were two very nice and obliging people who resided in Weaverham. She was an extremely large woman who took in sewing. Her husband was a small man, very pleasant and most polite. She possessed very large hands for a woman but this did not deter her from doing a good job of sewing. Her husband often came to the manor house to help in the grounds where he was sort of a handyman. In addition, if a large consignment of wool arrived from North Wales, Jack was there to help unload and stack it for the local merchants. Everyone turned a hand in Weaverham.

We Wyndhams were concerned about the number of villagers who could not read or write, so my dear mother took it upon herself to invite them up to the manor house, particularly on a lovely summer's day when she would place them on the grass. She would form words that were most difficult for them to learn, then she would invite one of them to write and she would help with the spelling. We were most afraid of people being served a notice and they would not know what that notice being served truly meant. They would place a thumb print or some other way to sign when it could place them in great danger, not knowing the seriousness of what they were reading or signing. Not all but some became excellent readers and it helped them to understand things better around them.

Chapter 8

Mr Cole

I must tell of Mr Cole, my dear friend. A bonny gentleman, heavy in build, he wore a cloak and long jacket with metal buttons. Moreover, I recall he wore his hair behind his ears, forming a ponytail, pantaloon trousers and hide stockings that were wrapped around his boots, to keep out the cold. Poor dear Mr Cole – he worked a small foundry in Weaverham making and forming metal for swords and rods to produce a contraption for fitting around the saddle on pins; rich embroidery was placed underneath, but first it was lined with a form of hide. He was so skilled in his work that King Charles II heard of him. I am afraid to say that Mr Cole wanted nothing to do with Charles II, for the reason that he was a very cruel and selfish ruler indeed.

However, the king put pressure on him to work for him. If Mr Cole had declined to work for the king, he and his poor family would have suffered, especially his wife who might have been killed to set an example to Mr Cole and other villagers of Weaverham. It did upset me to see a dear friend used in this way and I have full knowledge of the dreadful way he was treated. He worked so hard for the king, without a thank you or acknowledgement of any kind.

Other people suffered also; the king demanded that babes in arms were to be seized from their mothers and taken to him to be reared as workers for the king. And as these little ones grew up, they were heavily burdened with work that only a fit and strong man could cope with.

Mr Cole formed an alliance with the king solely to protect those people who were suffering because of this dreadful ruler. He bore witness to many harrowing things that were to haunt him for the rest of his earthly life.

Even while Mr Cole was working at his foundry he could hear the screams, of the poor people being beaten by the soldiers. He asked one soldier why they did this. The answer that came back was, 'If we do not beat the villagers to make them work harder, we shall be given an even harsher treatment on the order of the king; we have our orders and so we must carry them out to the full.' Mr Cole was filled with horror and decided that he must work harder to protect these poor beleaguered people.

Charles II was unfortunately unable to give love; he did not comprehend what true love contained. He relished in the glory of being cruel and, without emotion, he loved to control those who could not defend themselves. He also seemed to be a king lacking in intelligence, might I say. Never did people see any ruler go to such extremes, taxing everything in sight; the poor people could not pay these very heavy taxes which led to starvation and people being thrown into a debtors' prison. We witnessed many deaths of people who did not survive the terrible beatings or simply died of malnutrition. This broke Mr Cole's heart, and particularly when he tried to save a little child being snatched from its mother to be sent to serve this selfish king.

Charles II did not have one ounce of respect for ladies; he was very loose with his morals, I am afraid. Women became playthings to keep him amused and any offspring were simply not recognised – they became outcasts. Death came swiftly to him and yet we all pitied him in a way. At least we all helped each other in great love and compassion and dear Mr Cole was looked upon by the villagers as a protector and what you would call in your time a father figure. He gave so much to the villagers; they gained strength from him in many ways. Yet the king nearly worked this poor man to death; after Charles died Mr Cole was given the strength to go on and live for quite a long time, but these harsh memories did never leave him.

I remember a lovely person in Weaverham who served Mr and Mrs Cole whom I have mentioned already; her name was Lenora and she was always kept very busy indeed in the Cole household. She wore a dress down to her ankles of very heavy material and she always wore her bonnet surrounded by frills. Lenora was a lady of five foot eight, very tall for the ladies of my time, but she served them well. She also understood the important job that Mr Cole carried out in Weaverham and took care of his needs to the full. Mrs Cole was a heavy lady but a beautiful kind soul; she did many good works for Weaverham. She would hold small meetings with the ladies of the village, to see what they could do to improve things for the villagers. One favourite thing they loved doing was baking bread and cakes to help the poor. The Coles breathed new life into the village and helped to raise people's spirits; they were so loved and respected by the villagers. I do remember to this day the house that the Coles lived in. It was a wooden house but it had a fine quality about it; the structure was made up of wood, straw and sand packed so tightly. It was, as you would call today, open plan. There was a pleasant nook fireplace; a hook was attached for kitchen implements and also to hold the cauldron. Mr Cole had stencil painted pictures on the wooden panels of deep blue and gold. In addition, on the wall a picture hung of his grandfather, called Charles. Mr Cole incidentally was a very fine portrait artist. He even painted his own dear wife and it was quite charming. I do remember a beautiful low sideboard with carved figures surrounding this lovely piece of furniture. Also in the room there was a small wooden stool with splayed out legs; a ring supported the bottom of the stool, which was fashioned from a beer barrel; the legs were rather thick. On the kitchen table stood a wooden jug, with large handles, used for ale and, placed around the jug, was a set of wooden cups almost fashioned into oval shapes. These drinking cups were for the guests to drink their ale from. Mr and Mrs Cole loved to tell a true story to people, of the day a strange visitor arrived at their door.

The stranger they loved to talk about was no other than Rob Roy. He was directed to the Cole household and declared the reason for his visit by saying that he had ridden by horse from Scotland on hearing stories from travellers of the sufferings of the people of Weaverham. His conscience had led him to seek Weaverham himself, to find out the truth of all the atrocities he had heard of. Mr and Mrs Cole welcomed him and told him everything that they had experienced themselves at the hands of the puritans, and he seemed to be moved by the stories. While in Weaverham, he visited the tavern where Thomas was murdered, but he was very psychic and mediumistic; he felt a great unease in the tavern and did not stay long. Rob Roy had a pigtail tied with strips of material. He wore a three cornered hat and pantaloons of a black material with dark brown strapped layers of material made from hide tied around his ankles. He wore large shoes with gold coloured buckles and he displayed a thick beard. He told the Coles of weather changes in Scotland, which ranged from severe cold to extreme wet and damp conditions, in quick succession. He said that he had never experienced such severe weather changes.

Unfortunately, he declared that it brought an outbreak of tuberculosis and it was rampant. All they could do was to bathe the people's heads when they were delirious, and sweating. They had a great knowledge of herbs and they utilised this knowledge to try to help the poor souls who were dying of this dreadful illness. Some of the berries they squashed and made a juice for sick people to drink. He told us that many survived, but also many died. He told them that he did not know what caused this strange illness, so all the people who were stricken by tuberculosis came up with one positive answer that, to their knowledge, the strange illness was God's will and his way of punishing them for past sins.

Rob Roy was a fascinating character and we in Weaverham learned from this powerful man. One thing stood out about him; he had great compassion for the villagers of Weaverham and for the poor souls he left behind in Scotland.

Peace seemed to reign over Weaverham for a little while after the king's death and people started to rebuild after all the plundering they had suffered from. Where I now reside in the spirit world, I do see dramatic changes about to take place in your world, some good, and some bad.

Chapter 9

Weaverham, the first Orphanage

Nevill Marley was a very good archer and we would often travel with him deep into the Cheshire countryside to practise. The villagers were taught well and they felt safe because of this type of weapon. A large stake of wood would be driven into the ground and a papier-mache cross would be then mounted upon it for the archers to aim at. It was good for the local men to learn this skill simply because it was a silent way of attack. If they came across puritan soldiers in the forest, they could attack in silence and make a quick getaway, without anyone hearing any noise. They found it quick and effective.

I would only fight with my dagger or sword in total defence. I fought Angus Larchwood but this was forced upon me for I had to prevent him and his band from killing the king. My king loved to wear hats of different sorts with wonderful plumes. I remember, whenever I greeted him, he would say to me, 'Wyndham, do you like my hat?'

I would reply, 'Yes, Charles, you look quite regal.' On hearing this remark he would smile. However, it saddened me for, in the 17th century and much further on; people would kill beautiful birds so they could use their plumage. I loved birds. I would walk on my lands listening to their beautiful songs each day. I do hope I have not made Charles feel guilty by this remark; at least he did not kill the birds himself.

Quite a while after Moembah and his band of murderers had ransacked our village, there came to settle among the villagers a lovely kind gentleman by the name of Marten Couledge. He was told of the terrible atrocities that had taken place, and how many little children had been left orphaned. The puritans had killed their parents in cold blood showing no mercy whatsoever. Many of the older children were left to beg on the streets. It was dreadful. These soldiers did not deserve to carry the name of puritan. Marten Couledge was twenty-seven years of age and he had saved what money he had. He immediately realised that he must do something for these poor children some of whom suffered mental scarring also, after seeing their beloved parents killed by those barbarians.

Marten was a young man of great kindness. He sat thinking deeply what he should do to help these little ones. He decided to ask as many villagers as possible to help him build something to house these children. Many volunteered and did not want payment. With the help of Marten, they set about building a large hut which took them three weeks to complete. He felt so happy with the work that he rewarded the men with gold coins. I suppose one could say that this was the first known orphanage ever to be built for abandoned children.

There came also into the village a lady called Eliza Siorsedoir who had travelled from another land, trying to escape a plague. She wore a long plain type of dress but she loved to wear fancy bonnets. She also was horrified at what she had heard, the children starving, covered in mud and filthy dirty. This made Eliza cry. She at once volunteered her services to Marten and they worked so hard together. Marten had a good friend who was a saddler, Jon Will, and this good man made shoes and boots for these poor children.

A tiny baby who had lost its parents to the puritans was taken as their own by a couple who could have no children. They were Shelaise Petifer, aged thirty-two, and her husband of thirty-seven years and they were amazed that the little child had survived such a terrible ordeal. They called her Honor. Eliza eventually married Marten in 1690 and she did feed these little ones; she baked pies and made barley bread and the children learned to love Eliza dearly. When Marten and his wife did not have any more room for orphans, many kind villagers took the children in to their own homes. The villagers did their best to try to educate the children but, alas, these people lacked education themselves. Schools became law much later on; it proved most difficult for these poor orphans for they badly needed to be taught. The villagers spoke of Marten as a saviour perhaps sent by God to save these beautiful children.

Life was cheap at that time and villagers got used to seeing friends that they grew up with being dragged off to the dungeon to rot. Even young women, who became pregnant outside the confines of marriage, were treated badly after the birth. If the child survived the young women were publicly whipped to set an example to others. Young men rarely married before the age of thirty – if they survived to that age. People did not live long after the age of forty. They had to prove that they owned some sort of house or shelter to live in and held down some sort of job to keep a wife, who was of child bearing age. Many of our children were stillborn because of the lack of good food and sanitation.

In Weaverham, we had a panel of citizens, upright and what you in your time would call decent and upstanding; two local judges selected them and these people would sit on the panel when taxes would be decided. One judge in particular was called Bertram Hillman a very kind gentleman considering he held the position of judge; everyone in Weaverham had respect for him for he was fair and just and held the villagers at heart. The judge had a daughter who was so pretty. Her dark hair was piled on top of her head while the rest cascaded into ringlets each side of her head. For our time she was unusually tall at five foot seven, and beautiful, slim, with a tiny waist. She loved to wear green and her dresses were of the loveliest of silks, with a full bustle. She wore the most beautiful of necklaces provided by her father. Her name was Rebecca Hillman. At the age of three months she lost her mother, Hannah, through death.

She lived in the countryside with her father but all she did was sit and daydream. People used to be mistaken when they saw Rebecca for she had a strong resemblance to her mother. As time went by she developed tuberculosis and took to her bed; an older lady would assist bathing her poor head, as she lay in bed delirious and so very ill. Her father would never allow her to take up an occupation as she was a judge's daughter and he earned sufficient money to keep them both in the manner that they were both accustomed to.

A young gentleman who served the king at court fell in love with Rebecca, and requested her hand in marriage. Fate took a hand – this dashing young courtier called Petrey was not to be her husband as Rebecca died at the age of twenty-eight years on the 16th April 1672. Petrey was heartbroken, She suffered the worst of the illness for three weeks with intense fever.

Rebecca and her father had a Jewish background. Although her father was a respected judge, he did not command the great respect that his colleague who sat with him on the panels. However, no matter, the majority of the people loved them for the very kind people they were and people proved to be helpful and friendly in a most genuine way.

I do find it rather sad that wonderful kind people, like Judge Hillman and his daughter, had to endure the stigma of having a different background and, sadly, this is still the case in your world today. Yet Rebecca and her father found it in their hearts to forgive people, and her father contributed so much to Weaverham for being without malice, and fair in his judgement of people.

They were, I am sad to say, a very tragic family. Judge Hillman ended his days missing his lovely daughter so very much because, when he gazed at her on the days she was well, he could see a perfect mirror image of his dear wife, Hannah.

The illness of tuberculosis that Rebecca died from was rife in my time; many people suffered from severe chest conditions and we did not have the medical knowledge that your world has today. Limbs were lost; if they became badly infected, gangrene usually set in and the poor soul lost a limb through this. In addition, people suffered from blood conditions; where the doctor could not bring about a cure, leeches were used on the patient. Through your modern technology and x-ray machines, people's limbs can now be saved. It is truly a wonderful invention that I have learned of in my world. We had many people suffering from smallpox in those days.

Our asylums were also overcrowded with those poor souls who, unfortunately, most of the time were rejected by society and their families. All they needed was counselling and help given to them over their worries, caused through living under stressful conditions making them go a little off balance. Nevertheless, with a little bit of understanding and loving care they could have resumed a normal life in society. The poor misunderstood people who were diagnosed as possessed by the devil, provided an easy way out for the authorities who threw them into a dungeon to rot away and die listening to other inmates shouting and screaming who usually were the genuine cases of mental illness. None of them saw the light of day.

I do remember in Weaverham a most skilful gentleman who was a surgeon of my time; his name was Marcus Wolsey. He was clever in his diagnosis; the only problem being that he lacked the facilities to work with. He seemed to have an uncanny knowledge of the illness of each patient and people learned to trust him wholeheartedly. He always worked hard to try to find a way of curing the patient without amputation of any sort. Many of the surgeons would take it upon themselves to remove the arm, leg, whatever the case maybe, without trying some other way to help the patient first. This was not the case with Marcus Wolsey.

The Wyndhams tried to help in replacing some of the houses destroyed by the puritans. We found craftsmen willing to help to build up such houses destroyed by fire. Our houses in the village looked like stables the way they were constructed, from timber and sectioned off into small rooms. If set on fire they were apt to burn fiercely. If a family lost their home through fire we tried to help them as much as we could. They could not replace their home once it was destroyed because of lack of money and resources. Being lord of the manor had its advantages when this type of catastrophe happened.

Sometimes we experienced some merriment in Weaverham particularly when Cornelius paid our village a visit for he came to our village square to make people laugh. I suppose that in your time you would call him an actor, as we would call him in my time a jester, of sorts. He would act out charades and sometimes he would ask for a volunteer but usually people would be shy. He would not of course be allowed to joke about politics or the puritans, even the king, or anything that might be sensitive. He would wear a very large papier-mache nose and would colour his cheeks red with berries. People would gather around and small children also and laugh at him most heartily. He would speak in riddles and the townsfolk would have to guess what he was referring to. Cornelius greeted the person who guessed correctly with a majestic bow. This made a welcome change to hear the local villagers laugh, even some of the hard drunken puritan soldiers laughed for even on merry times they were never off duty.

Because travellers from outside Weaverham came to offer sympathy and compassion, this gave enormous strength to those who suffered at the hands of the puritans; it gave them the courage to rebuild not only lives but also homes. Many of the villagers were in wonderment at the very thought of the likes of Rob Roy travelling to Weaverham from as far afield as Scotland. We were proud of our people and the way in which they gathered great strength from each other working together. They did rise and start to rebuild the village. Every village round and about conducted their affairs differently from each other at that time. Yet, this did not deter them from joining to help their neighbours from the next village.

I do recall a rich merchant called Michael Finch. He also had heard from travellers about the plight of Weaverham, and he travelled from the town of Manchester to offer his services. He lived in a large town house in that city in which many rich merchantmen lived; this gentleman did not offer his services for business favours. He possessed a genuine interest in what had taken place and offered a substantial amount of money to help to rebuild the village. Those who were in charge of collecting taxes and court payments gratefully accepted the kind and generous offer of this gentleman and the money was put to good use. Some buildings had been completely gutted by fire.

Life proved to be most hard if you were poor. That is why I thanked God on every morning that I awakened. In addition, my thoughts reached out to these poor souls and I would gaze around my beautiful manor house, with its rich tapestries and beautiful paintings adorning the walls. My favourite picture was that of my mother and father standing before our beautiful fireplace, she wearing a most beautiful flowing dress and father standing next to her looking so content and happy. I would often reflect on why I deserved all these rich trappings and other poor wretches were foraging like wild animals for any scrap of food they could find. I could never comprehend why I was so privileged.

I was very privileged indeed to have such a loving family. Mother and father were so devoted to each other and, as I have mentioned before, we had lovely gatherings of friends. The solstice was a great time of rejoicing, may I say. I was extremely proud of my parents in that life of the 17th century and I find it so wonderful that my pride of them extends into this life, for the valuable work they did.

In addition, I am so grateful for the wonderful support I have had from Irene, helping Mary in the writing of this book. Never in my wildest dreams did I ever think that I would be communicating back and forth with my beloved parents and daughter Anna who in this life is Irene. I give thanks each day for the powers that be, which ordained that all this should take place.

When I think back to my brother Thomas, he often took dangerous risks when he frequented the tavern drinking. I would become quite anxious particularly after dark if Thomas had not yet returned. I do think that he drank heavily to try to blank out his conscience. Yet, the tavern was a most dangerous place, because of the many puritan spies.

I often had the task of collecting him from the tavern in my coach, assisted by my able coachman. I suppose it looked quite suspicious to the local inhabitants. Thomas was a gentleman and it was very rare indeed especially in the village to witness the gentry drinking with travellers and locals. It would prove to be a great curiosity to some.

It caused so much unhappiness when Thomas was accused of the murder of Margaret and Anna. I never envisaged ever forgiving my brother. It was an even greater burden to be accused of a second murder and robbery also. Whatever pain and suffering he caused to us Wyndhams, he did not deserve to be blamed for something he had not carried out, and it did hurt us so much. However I do feel so much happier now and content from where I reside. I have indeed forgiven my brother; I cannot imagine what my life would have been like if I had carried all that terrible bitterness inside me. It is indeed a lovely feeling to have that courage, to forgive in one's heart.

Weaverham created many characters, but they all found their own little jobs to do, like Samual Irvine who tended the graves at the church. He would tidy up the graves by removing dead leaves and any rubbish that may have accumulated during the week. His task was also to look out for vagabonds, for they would try to sleep behind the graves, and watch that they did not stray into the church. These vagabonds became many in number; most of them had been abandoned when young because their families could not provide for them. Some used to rely on poaching or living on their wits; they would try to obtain a few scraps of food from any villager kind enough to help them. However, if found out the villagers faced many hours in the stocks having rotten vegetables and other things thrown at them.

Chapter 10

The Death of the Manor House and Myself

I remember in my time the cruelty and barbarism that took place' there was scarcely a day go by when no one was hanged at the tavern. We had puritan spies who would frequent the tavern listening for some poor wretch to speak out of turn. In addition, we had those local people who would betray their neighbour for a small reward. The only difference was that if they were caught and it was proven then they in turn would be swinging from the elm tree themselves. Therefore the small reward did not do that person any good; I am afraid to say these where barbaric times.

The manor house was eventually destroyed by marauding monks who travelled from Ireland; they wished to gain control over the property and land because they wanted to gain a foothold in the north of England. They did not want a protestant king so they established themselves in Cheshire to strengthen that part of England, which was closest to Ireland. They brought terror with them, torching everything in sight, taking land and property by brute force; they wore sinister black cloaks and gauze like masks across their faces. We received fair warning from a runner and we took what we could carry and escaped – all except my nephew Damon who was the recorder at the Wheatsheaf tavern. These barbaric monks raised the manor house to the ground and Damon was killed. He did not leave quickly enough as he was helping two young boys who were guests at the manor; the elder was only eleven years old. With his aid the two boys escaped but, unfortunately, it was Damon's time for he perished in the fire. This dreadful act took place in 1676. We had to move swiftly and silently so as not to be seen otherwise I dread to think what fate would await us. Our property was destroyed because, although we were of the catholic faith, we had many protestant friends and openly supported King Charles. I looked behind me only to see properties ablaze and people screaming and begging for mercy. I shuddered and wondered what had befallen our family and the rest of the inhabitants in Weaverham.

My household staff, the two boys and a young servant with her baby escaped with myself. Her poor dear husband was caught up trying to fend off the perpetrators who torched the manor; I am sad to say that they killed this young man. Fortunately we had good strong horses and we rode at great speed. I did seek shelter with loyal friends. We learned later that these marauding monks had decided to make Weaverham their permanent home which meant that we had to move on. After losing our beautiful and dearly beloved manor, we lost an even finer treasure in my nephew Damon, bless his soul.

I must mention that the marauding monks, although they crossed over from Ireland, were not Irish but were in fact French. These French monks carried out such cruel acts before they torched the ground and the manor house that we so loved. They burned down homes and murdered the local children to keep the population down in the future by prevent those dear little children from growing up, marrying and so producing children themselves.

I managed to escape to Broughton Manor where William Broughton, my dear friend, offered us shelter. He was of the protestant faith and a gentleman of great sincerity. Oh, how he took care of us, enabling me to rest my weary body.

William Broughton was blessed with a beautiful wife who did sing for us to lift our spirits; she possessed a beautiful voice. Her name was Annalita and she and her husband loved each other so much it was pure delight to see. They had a lovely son called James who was strong in character; I liked this boy. James proved to be a good horseman. He had a sister, a lovely child, so pretty around the eyes; her name was Helena and she was thirteen years of age.

My servants and I were treated so kindly by William and his family; he was a very kind man of large stature and a big heart to match. He knew and understood the heartache that had befallen our family and I felt deeply indebted to him. Never have I ever experienced such kindness from a fellow human being. I was tired and weary; my thoughts drifted back to the time that poor dear Margaret and Anna had been murdered when I considered taking my own life through grief.

It was with great sadness that the day I did flee the manor house after the monks torched it to the ground, I realised that I would never look upon the beautiful paintings again of my dear father, mother, wife Margaret, daughter Anna and myself. They were priceless. We had built up the manor with lovely tapestries and works of art, but also the most precious of things was love. In happy times the house was full with warmth and love and anyone who stepped inside was heartily welcomed by the Wyndham family.

As I looked back with great sadness I reflected on those happy times that we all shared. Now it was in ruins. I felt it would only be a matter of time when I would leave this earth for good.

While staying at Broughton Manor, I had time to sit and reflect back to the days when Thomas and I were young children along with my sister. Thomas even from childhood had a strong willpower and he often resented it if I were on the receiving end of too much attention from mother and father. He would sulk for days. One fine quality we shared was when we walked on our land together as brothers. Taking in the beauty of the countryside and we delighted in listening to the birds and having lively conversation with each other. I loved to dwell on this most pleasant of thoughts.

The marauding monks were acting independently for their own cause and the puritans took advantage of this. The puritans disliked William Broughton because he was a close friend of mine. The puritans seized the opportunity to hang him, because of the kindness shown to me by William.

My dear and loyal friend who offered me shelter and safety, William Broughton, was to be reported to the puritan soldiers for helping me when the marauding French monks torched the ground and Wyndham Manor. The puritan soldiers arrived at Broughton Manor looking for William and dragged poor dear William to the village square, where they did hang him, bless his soul. I managed to escape from Broughton Manor.

Earlier this year, while reviewing the book, I asked Patrick Wyndham to explain the time difference between leaving the manor after the monks had torched it to the ground and his death that he had recorded as 1682. Patrick answered by saying,

I come to you, mother, with a heavy heart full of shame and sadness. I did not tell you the truth and, at this stage, I have been told by the guardians that I must make amends, for my future progression. You must know the truth.

I was not killed in 1682 but in 1678. This part of my life started in 1676. The reason is that, when leaving William Broughton to his fate, I felt I had let my dear friend down by escaping as quickly as possible to the Welsh border. I arrived tired and exhausted, my heart feeling as if it would explode.

There I met up with a dear friend called Jon Adams. Although he was a much older man, he resembled me in looks and stature. Jon had devised a plan to help me to escape but, before we could put this plan into action, the soldiers caught up with me. We rode away as fast as we could but we both received gunshot wounds. Jon knew of a cave with running water nearby where we could hide. On checking our wounds, I was not seriously hurt but Jon's injury was more severe. He told me he had sent word to the elders in what is now called Colwyn Bay and word had come back that we were to travel there by boat.

Jon unfortunately had consumption and did not have long to live, coupled with the injury he had received. He suggested we should exchange clothing and horses so as to give me a much better chance of escape. As he was too ill to travel far, he gave me instructions to find the elders. We heard the soldiers searching the caves in the area where we were hiding. We decided to make a break; at this point the soldiers heard us and gave chase. I looked back to see Jon's horse shot and go beneath him. To my shame, I had to leave him. He was a wonderful friend and as a brother to me. Jon was killed and the soldiers took his body back to Weaverham and buried him in my stead.

Since I have resided in these realms I have suffered thoughts of shame and remorse because my dear friends took my place to save me. The puritans were very cunning and devious and suspected it was not I that was buried in the family grave. So after I had managed to escape from them, they continued their endeavours to find me.

It was made easier for them because they employed many spies. Although I was wounded I managed to meet up with the gentleman who was to provide me with a boat. He knew I was desperate and he took a good payment for the use of the boat that was used to ferry goods to different places. I arrived in the place called Colwyn Bay to be met by the elders. They hastily took me to a secret underground cavern so I could rest, eat, and have my wound tended too. The elders where so kind and loyal to me that I shall never forget their kindness. I stayed with them for just less than two years in the place they called the settlement. After that length of time, I thought I might be safe to travel back to my beloved Weaverham, but this is were I made a fatal mistake. I bade goodbye to my faithful friends the elders, who were called Samuel Pullet, Harvey Mannelit, and Paolo Sirenguilo, a Spaniard. Samuel Pullet lived to the age of sixty-one years; he passed on on 1st January 1679. Harvey Mannelit passed on on 27th May 1680, aged sixty-three. In addition, Paolo Sirenguilo also passed on in 1680, on 29th October.

I remember feeling so sad leaving them behind. I had come to know them and love them as very special friends, equal to brothers. However, I mounted my horse and began to ride once more towards the Welsh border. Little did I know that some poor settlers had been paid handsomely to spy and to inform the puritans if they should see me heading towards the border. One man was placed among them who knew my face. These peasants took payment because they were very poor and needed to buy food for their families. A man started to pursue me on horseback. I rode faster and faster until I heard a shot and felt a searing pain close to my spine. Then he fired twice more: one shot grazed my right side then another one found its target close to my heart. I rode faster until I came to a barn where I dismounted with blood pouring from my wounds. I staggered into the barn and, feeling great pain and tiredness, I started to lapse into unconsciousness. When I heard voices, I opened my eyes only to see puritan soldiers and one man whom I recognised as one called Alun Soadins. He was the very same man who had followed me and shot me three times. I was shocked because this man once served as a soldier in the army of King Charles I. He did not present himself well to the king, was often found drunk and he often caused problems even for the ladies in his life. He joined Charles's army as a boy soldier but he always presented problems for those who where in command of him. I then felt myself passing into a faint because of intense pain and loss of blood. It was at that moment that one of the soldiers shot me through the head. I can still smell the stench of ale permeating from their foul mouths. My life ended in July 1678.

I suppose this way of dying was far better and more dignified than what befell my dear loyal friend William, hung in public before those drunken puritans and those bloodlust people who took delight in watching hangings.

Those puritan soldiers placed my body in a cart and took me back to Weaverham, but at least they allowed me to be buried with my dear family.

What a wonderful surprise to find that I was floating in my spiritual body, feeling free at last from all the pain and suffering I had endured as Patrick Wyndham, to be rewarded by feeling the love of my wife Margaret and all those who had gone before me. Oh what joy! I passed to the realms of light, the spirit world or whatever you wish to call it. To my great surprise I learned that I had only shed my physical body and I felt very much alive in what I was to learn was my spiritual body.

Chapter 11

After my Passing

Weaverham at that time seemed to attract settlers from different places; also, it brought about many changes that we had to get used to. Never did I think that such a quiet and picturesque place would attract people from other lands.

When in the spirit world I was fortunate to witness the changes in Weaverham that lifted my heart. For I had always felt fear and sadness for those poor people I had been forced to leave behind by those puritans who had taken my life. In 1692 a lovely gentleman called Mr Bromwell arrived in Weaverham bringing with him such colour so badly needed to cheer the citizens of our village. Mr Bromwell was a most wonderful artist and took great delight in painting fruits, blueberries and such, that one would think the fruit could be plucked and eaten straight out of the picture. The colours he used in the pictures lifted people's spirits to great heights after so much extreme sadness had been brought into their lives.

It was wonderful to see new blood being brought into the village; men came to settle and started to rebuild those buildings which had been torched to the ground and plundered by the soldiers. A Mr Kent arrived to take up the post as judge of the people. I passed over in 1678 and I can say wholeheartedly that my heart remains there until this very day, in the beautiful countryside of Cheshire and in particular Weaverham.

I was overjoyed yet saddened in a way, when I learned from this side of life that my beloved Weaverham had been transformed and rebuilt, after the savagery of the puritans, by a wealthy gentleman called John Glen. Saddened only because I was not there to witness this in my physical body; he rebuilt and replenished the whole of the area. He asked nothing of the local people only their support of what he had done; this gentleman was well travelled to foreign parts. Moreover, he brought to Weaverham much wealth in materials, which furnished the need for very fine clothing indeed. This material was also a great deal warmer for when the snow did fall heavily it brought much needed warmth to the body. He also brought many fine silks for the ladies.

John Glen had a lovely wife called Venetia; he brought her from overseas. They travelled to many islands together and they were devoted to each other; he and his wife were both kind spiritual people. It made me so wonderfully happy to know that the place that we fought so hard for in the 17th century was now calm and peaceful. In addition, not one villager would have to live in fear of being dragged off to the dungeon. The birds sang once more and people greeted each other with smiling happy faces. The men wore fine clothing and the ladies looked feminine. What a tremendous change from the poor wretches I did see wearing sackcloth and rags, so undernourished they could scarcely stand up. Oh how happy this made me to see such a wonderful transformation.

Even now I reflect and think back to all those very brave villagers who lost families and their homes but never did I witness anyone being selfish. Even under the most severest of attacks from the soldiers, everyone turned their hand to helping each other with great love and loyalty, disregarding their own safety. So you can imagine my joy at hearing that Weaverham had risen from the ashes, thanks to John Glen. I still shed a tear or two for my beloved Cheshire.

At the beginning of the 1800s, Weaverham slowly attracted more outsiders. Mr Simons and his dear wife Elizabeth with their son Michael came in 1882. They brought some colour to the village by opening up a small shop selling ladies' ribbons in pretty colours, warm winter shawls, satin material for the ladies to make dresses and all manner of things for the local ladies to buy. Michael amused himself with a large wooden hoop, which no doubt his father had fashioned from an ale keg. The boy used a wooden stick to make the hoop roll down the village street. The village children found this so amusing and they would fall about in fits of laughter watching this boy perform with this wonderful toy. The boy's cheeks would take on the deep blush of a fully ripened apple at the thought that he had encouraged an audience of young children. Mr Simons had no doubt created this toy to help the young boy to adjust into his new environment and to take away any boredom that might set in with him. The ladies of the village were well pleased to see new blood brought in from outside, and ladies haberdashery was welcomed in this tiny shop, which also gave them the excuse to call in to meet with other ladies to speak about the gossip of the day. Young Michael made many friends particularly when he let other boys take turns at rolling this wonderful toy down the village street.

It is most interesting to note that Weaverham seemed to draw many outsiders into the village; people seemed to be drawn to the place as if by a magnet. The good thing is that most of those adventurers who came managed in their own way to contribute so much to the place. For some reason, it even attracted people from foreign lands; one family in 1692 even travelled from the Americas by ship. The young lady of the family was overjoyed to have been able to travel such a great distance in that time.

It is a great pleasure for me to look upon these scenes of joy from where I now reside, to see children playing in my beloved village and not having to live in fear any more. It does sadden me to think that our dear little children did not have this privilege but, no matter, times have changed. I can think of nothing more delightful than children's laughter, for children are quite innocent. That is why children must be taught from an early age to share whatever they have with each other, to give love freely and also to respect not only their parents but other adults. This prepares the child for adult life and, if the children are taught correctly, they in turn when they marry and have children of their own, will pass on this love and knowledge to their little ones making a much better world to live in.

Weaverham finally struggled to its feet in 1899 when a very fine gentleman arrived in the village. His name was Mr Tomlin and he was a banker, aged 35 years. He took a good look around Weaverham. He liked what he saw so he decided to settle down and set about opening premises to carry out his banking. Many people became curious and interested in this dashing flamboyant character; he set about vetting all the young ladies of the village looking for a potential wife to share his new life. His eyes cast a glance on young pretty Annabelle; she had long thick blonde hair, beautiful skin, and she was so petite just like a doll. Mr Tomlin towered over Annabelle for he was five foot ten inches tall.

He was a formidable gentleman; the villagers honoured him but some feared him because of his importance and his size. He did not carry too much weight, though he wore a moustache and beard; his hair was long but somewhat curled up underneath, tied back, and he wore a hat that was specially made for him. Mr Tomlin wore the finest of cloaks about his shoulders; his shirt was of the finest silk on both sides of his chest. He wore fancy buttons and bows down the front of his shirt and baggy trousers braided with silks which all made him a dashing figure to look upon. He finally proposed to Annabelle; they married and produced six boys and a girl, though poor Annabelle was so ill over the last child she nearly lost her life, but she pulled through.

Annabelle was very tired after having so many children; the ladies of the village proved to be a good help to her and the rest of her children. They were always on hand to help with the little ones so she could rest. Mr Tomlin acquired a grey pony for the children and they loved it so. The dear little animal served the family for many years; the villagers looked upon this family in wonderment at the way Annabelle and her husband looked upon each other with great love and did their very best for the children. They were such a loving family and people would talk about how Annabelle was besotted by her husband even as the years rolled by. He brought wealth to Weaverham and that encouraged more people to come and settle.

This gentleman's bold venture caused the village to prosper. Cheshire started to expand as other bankers and rich people decided to move into the area and it became a very busy place indeed. Unfortunately not everyone who was enticed by the very pretty village was as honest and kind as dear Mr Tomlin and his lovely wife, but at least they themselves brought romance and goodness to the village. They reared seven lovely well-mannered children for all to see. It was a treat at Christmas time to see those little ones following behind dear Mr Tomlin carrying gifts to dear friends they had made in the pretty village of Weaverham, and they all looked blissfully happy to be with their father. Mr Tomlin was sixty-three years when he passed on, and his wife was sixty years when she passed; this was considered as old age.

When I finally made my transition to the spirit world and after I had taken a long rest, the guardians explained to me where I was. Of course I was surprised and shocked but they pointed out to me that it was important that I be shown flashbacks of the life I had inhabited on the earth plane. I saw everything of my life, the sadness and the joys of that life, in moving picture form. I explained to them that I felt a great sadness that no one would ever know the truth about the Wyndhams and especially what had happened to poor Thomas. I started to attend the great halls of learning, listening to eminent speakers, who had also lived on the earth plane before. I learned so much even how to speak in the plain English that you speak today, instead of conversing in old English.

To have to converse in plain English was to prove to be important for what next was to transpire, they the teachers who were appointed to me explained to me that permission had been granted from a higher source to fulfil my dream by putting things right, by writing the truth about the Wyndhams, to be finally read by people on the earth plane. Can you imagine my delight and happiness to be given this wonderful opportunity? But first it was explained to me that my dearly beloved mother, Lady Mariella Wyndham, had gone through another life on the earth plane along with Anna and my father. Anna was my daughter and Charles Wyndham my father. I was then told that I had to be most patient and would have to wait until my dear mother reached a certain stage in her life, before I was allowed to make my entrance.

I also had to wait until my dear mother, who is now Mary, was reunited with my father who in this life is Penry, and my daughter Anna, who in this life is Irene. All this had to take place before I could reveal to all three that this book was ordained by the spirit world to be written, the whole truth to be told. My dearly beloved mother honourably took on this task of writing the truth about our lives as the Wyndhams in the 17th century. These were barbaric times and yet it taught me a great deal. I saw many acts of kindness and bravery as well as the dreadful hardships of ordinary hard working people. In addition, we had eccentric characters in Weaverham that often made us chuckle and this took away the harsh reality of suffering under the watchful eyes of the puritans.

At last, I have now learned to forgive my twin brother Thomas for taking the lives of my dear ones. It is a most wonderful feeling to find forgiveness in one's heart as I do in forgiving him; it will make it far easier for him to progress in the realms of light, knowing in his heart that I have forgiven him. When the powers that be feel that Thomas is ready to be among us, I shall place my arms about him gladly and give him a brotherly hug, for I shall feel we are a family united once more.

Chapter 12

Thomas's Rescue

Having enjoyed a long rest after arriving in the realms of light, I was informed by my lovely guardian (or angel as you may wish to call him) that I had safely arrived into the next world, which consisted of beauty and light. I experienced so much love coming towards me. Later I was to learn that part of this love was being sent from my beloved wife Margaret, the beautiful soul I thought I had lost for ever. Can you imagine the great joy I felt! I then learned that my dear mother Lady Mariella Wyndham, my father Charles Wyndham and my beloved daughter Anna had been sent back to the earth plane to complete an important task that now I can reveal to you.

Over three hundred years passed before I made contact with my dear mother, who had to go through other lives. In addition, she had to experience sadness and pain in this life which conditioned her for the important work set out for her by the powers that be.

I learned too that my dear father and daughter had also experienced other lives to condition them for important work they had to carry out. My dear mother had married in this life to another but unfortunately that did not work out. The powers that be ordained that mother and father should meet again in this life and be joined up as husband and wife once more, and this took place in February 1997.

Dear Anna, my daughter, was born into this life as a wonderfully gifted medium; her name in this life is Irene. One beautiful sunny day in June 1998, my dear mother, who is named Mary in this life, visited Irene, whom she had known for over twenty years, with her husband in this life, Penry, who has this name because he is Welsh. I should say that Penry was my father Charles Wyndham, in my lifetime. Irene, Mary and Penry had finished having afternoon tea when I took it upon myself to present myself to them. I explained to Irene, who could see and hear me, that I had been waiting to contact Mary as it was ordained and written in the spirit world. At the appropriate time, I, Patrick Wyndham, was to let it be known to her that she had been given the important task of writing the truth in book form about the Wyndham family of that time.

Mary, Penry and Irene were very surprised and found it hard to believe but

Thomas Wyndham

74

Mary promised me that she would undertake the task of working with me through her mediumship in completing this important book. That very evening I made my presence known to Mary and she started to write under my guiding influence. After a couple of evenings of Mary writing, my brother unfortunately made his presence known and felt to Mary and me. Yes, this was my very same twin brother who had murdered Margaret and Anna on 19th September, 1658. I tried to make him leave because he was caught between the two worlds in limbo and should not have been with us.

Mary, too, tried to persuade Thomas to leave, explaining that he was earth-bound and that she and Irene would do everything within their power to help him. Thomas became very angry. Mary invited him to write down how he felt, and this is what he said:

'I, Thomas, will prevent you from writing this book for I am condemned. Mother, you do not know what they said about me, before they did hang me at the tavern.'

Mary replied, 'Thomas, you are not condemned, you are causing yourself to feel like a prisoner because of your own thought. Please go towards the light and help will be at hand for you, I promise you.'

With that remark Thomas became even more agitated and angry. He said again, 'I shall prevent you from writing this book.'

Mary then said to Thomas, 'I love you. I was your mother in that life. Do you love me?'

With that, Thomas replied, 'I do love you, mother dear, but I do not trust you.'

Mary that night retired to bed feeling saddened at what had taken place with Thomas. He was determined that he was going to stop her from writing the book at all costs. The next morning Mary called her friend Irene and explained to her what Thomas had said. Irene gasped in great surprise and explained to Mary that Thomas had paid her a visit also but he declared to Irene that he was most regretful and sorry for the trouble he had caused. He begged Irene for forgiveness, which she granted gladly. Mary was swift to explain that Thomas was trying to fool her. At the precise moment when Irene and Mary engaged in conversation, Thomas reappeared to Irene. He portrayed such anger and he shouted and threatened because we had found him out. At that point, I myself appeared to my brother and requested that he should leave and walk towards the light to seek help. At this, his anger became intolerable, so I left his presence. Irene ordered Thomas to leave and, in an instant, he was gone.

Mary and Irene became concerned for Thomas because they knew that if my brother did not take heed and seek help, he could interfere and seriously prevent the book from being written.

The very next day Mary and Irene decided to hold a rescue circle which must only be performed by qualified mediums of great experience. Mary and Irene organised the rescue for the following Friday. Mary had no sooner sat next to

Irene when Irene went quickly into trance. A loud voice broke the silence: it was Thomas who asked in a very loud voice, 'What are all these people doing here?' He was referring to three people who had arrived to give their support.

Mary replied, 'Do not worry about these people. They have come to support you and they send much love to you.'

Thomas's voice becoming louder and angrier, he then asked, 'Why do you forgive me when I am condemned?'

Mary replied, 'You are not condemned, Thomas; we love and support you. Please go towards the light. We are trying to help you.'

Mary then asked, 'Who am I, Thomas?' and he then replied in a low voice, 'Mother.' He then answered, 'You do not know what my so-called friends said about me. Why do you forgive me for I am a murderer?'

Mary replied, 'Because I love you. Thomas, go towards the light, for no one in this room is free of guilt. We also one day will have to atone for sins that we have committed.' Thomas turned his head away towards the left and Mary continued,'Thomas, do not turn away from me. Tell me please, who am I?'

The reply came back, 'Mother!'

Mary replied, 'Yes, it is. I am your mother and I do promise you that when I make my transition to the other side, I shall seek you out and I shall place my arms about you with such love.'

He said again, 'Why do you support me? I am truly condemned.'

Mary replied, 'We are all supporting you, Thomas, with great love. Please calm down. All will be well. Please leave gently and take my love with you.'

Thomas lowered his head and said, 'Please forgive me.' At this point he shouted, 'They have come! They are taking me away!' He meant the guardians from the realms of light.

Mary replied, 'They have come with much love and compassion. They will not harm you, so please go, Thomas, with peace and love in your heart. Go calmly.

As Mary repeated these words he shouted, 'Oh Momma!' He was gone.

With this very last statement from Thomas, Mary wept and felt a mother's love welling up inside her for poor unfortunate Thomas.

I must say that my dear brother Thomas is progressing splendidly and recently paid Mary, Penry and Irene a visit to thank them and to place his seal of approval in the writing of this book.

I desired to set the truth down for all to read. I lived all those years ago and witnessed the most barbaric of treatments of which I became one of the fatalities and losing my earthly life by being murdered by the puritans. I feel it gives people a much deeper insight into what really happened by one who actually lived through it and suffered by it. Reading a history book is not as truthful as listening to someone like myself who actually lived and breathed in this life. As I have mentioned before I would have laid down my life for King Charles I. I witnessed history taking place at first hand and we Wyndhams were very close

76

to the king. I would not be allowed from this side of life not to tell the whole truth as it has been ordained that this book will be written.

By giving the truth at first hand helps people to understand the trials and tribulations that we had to endure at that time. However, the wonderful thing about all this is that no matter who puts us through torture or takes our life, once you reach this side of life progress is open to everyone. The sooner you learn to forgive with your heart the person or persons who took your earthly life from you, they will progress far quicker. Also because of your forgiveness, you will progress far quicker because you have released all the hate and venom that you held for this person. I can vouch for that because I forgave those who killed Thomas and myself. The most important thing to me was to be able to forgive my brother for taking away my beloved wife and daughter. Does this make sense? I think so.

Chapter 13

My Emotional Journey to the Past

One lovely summer's day in July 1998, I visited Irene for, as I have explained before, she is now a medium and I asked her to visit Weaverham. I did not disclose my reasons for this, as I wanted the story to unfold in front of her eyes. The following week we embarked on our journey to Weaverham. Penry drove the car with Irene and Mary as passengers. In addition, of course I was an invisible passenger, but visible to Irene for she sees me very plainly indeed. I must say that I found Penry's car to be rather strange and frightening. Oh the speed that these monsters go! I remarked that day that I very much preferred a coach and horses – more dignified and a lot safer, may I add!

I directed Irene to a narrow lane in a place called Little Leigh. What a pretty place it was! The sun was shining and the birds were singing merrily. I was suddenly overcome with great emotion. I asked all three to step out of the car and to enter the field that was to the left of us. There was no gate, just hedging either side of this lush green field.

At once, Irene was filled with great emotion, saying she had been here before, and she broke into a run until she reached the far end of the field, where she could not venture any further. Mary followed slowly, then Penry; both were puzzled at Irene's apprehension and fear at entering the field. When they were finally all three standing together I spoke to Irene and asked her what she felt, and then I began using my energy to push her gently towards a certain spot on the field. She was slightly shocked at being pushed. Even Mary showed concern and at one point asked me why I was doing this.

I then replied to Irene that this was the spot that I found her and her mother on that fateful day, on 19th September 1658. Thomas had murdered them both. All three became emotional and a few tears were shed. They took some pictures of the field and I suggested that it was now time to leave. When all three were settled back in the car I directed Irene once more, until not too far away we came upon the lane were Wyndham Manor had once stood. My emotions took hold of me again.

I apologised to Irene because I was so very much overcome. I asked Irene to suggest to Penry that we must stay for just a few moments. On that very spot directly in front of us I had lived with my beloved family. It is now a farm. The building is newly erected, not the original building that we had occupied in the 17th century. My life flashed before me just for a fleeting second in my thoughts and, day dreaming, I felt I was back in that time. Oh the emotions that welled up inside me. When I had regained my senses I quickly asked Irene to direct Penry to drive away swiftly before I was taken over with my emotions once more. I remained quiet for the remainder of the journey.

My dear brother also showed great emotion when Irene, Mary and Penry returned to the tavern in Weaverham where poor Thomas was so cruelly beaten and murdered by hanging. He too had to endure and relive the events leading up to his death when he appeared to Irene in the tavern that day. It took great courage to return to that place to explain to Irene how he had died and to break the news to Mary that he had secretly married in St Mary's church in Weaverham. Because he had murdered Margaret and Anna, he was not yet allowed to meet up with his new wife in the spirit world until he had progressed and atoned for his deeds. I felt proud of my brother Thomas on that day, for this meant that he had decided to work towards progression but I realised the emotional pain he must have endured.

I smiled when I learned that Thomas, on entering the earth plane to speak to Mary and Irene, remarked to Irene, 'Why are you wearing men's breeches?'

She answered, 'Oh we ladies do now wear them.' Thomas. the poor soul, was quite taken aback at this answer. I myself am learning so much now about your lifetime and the wonderful inventions you do now possess. I do think your listening device is quite wonderful – I am now referring to the telephone.

I travelled back to Weaverham over a period of a few weeks to help Irene and Mary with the research of my family. It came as a great shock to me to see how the countryside I loved had changed. When I resided here so long ago, my own recollection was of seeing unspoilt beautiful countryside that had lovely lush green fields and pretty hedgerows. I loved to work the land – it brought me so much pleasure. The horses worked so hard, so graciously, such a majestic animal, and such good company when the day was long.

I do remember so vividly walking on those beautiful grasses, or fields of grass as you would call them in your time, with my dear brother Thomas, when we were young men, hands clasped behind our backs.

Even now, that beautiful thought does enter my head, from time to time, of how happy Thomas and I were walking upon those fields. Even as children we took great delight in the beautiful countryside of Cheshire, sheer delight to us. I do remember those little wild creatures you would call cats. They would come around the manor house seeking food when the weather took on a chill. My darling daughter Anna, when she was quite small, loved to cradle one in her arms, which caused me great alarm in case the creature sank its claws into her.

I now realise how strong our emotions are; even after a few hundred years; those strong bonds still do exist. The places we have lived, the people we have loved, and the dreadful experiences we may have had to endure. My dearly beloved mother, who is now Mary in this life, may have a different face and a different body. However, my love for her, for Irene who was my daughter, and Penry who was my father, has never changed even in this life. When I draw close to Mary when she is writing this book, I do feel her love and respect for me, and she feels a tremendous love and respect that I feel for her. Therefore, this perfect attunement helps us to work well together in harmony and peaceful contentment. I feel so blessed to be reunited with those who played an important part in my life in 17th century England.

Those people on the earth plane, who read this book, will wonder why it was so long before this book was written. I shall explain to you. When we step into our spiritual body, which is a replica of our physical body, this is in fact the real you. This enables you to go forward and live on in a higher dimension that is an extension of this physical world of yours. You will experience the sensation of feeling light and happy that you will not suffer the earthly pain that you experienced before you left your earthly body. A guardian, or even a member of your family, who you knew to be passed over, will come to you and explain to you that you now reside in the spirit world because some people on first passing over are confused as to where they are.

When it is explained to people what has happened to them, they start to feel relieved, because great care is taken and great love is given to the new arrival. In addition, they become anxious to meet other members of their family and friends who have made this transition. Thomas, after he was beaten and hung in the tavern, was very confused indeed but the great difference was that Thomas had been told that, after he was hung he would be condemned into eternity, by those whom carried out his execution.

Poor dear Thomas, in his terrified mind, truly believed that this would take place. Those lovely souls on our side of life tried to explain to Thomas that he would have a chance to progress and atone for the murders, without being condemned, but he would not listen because he did not trust anyone at that point.

My dear mother volunteered, as I have already explained, to come back into this life, because the guardians on this side of life knew that. Thomas would be a prisoner of his own mind and would refuse to listen to anyone. Therefore, he remained earthbound between the two worlds for over three hundred years, living in torment and great fear. I had to wait until Mary was born into this life and be able to meet up with my father later on, and Irene, so I could come through and make myself known to them, as I have. The point that I am trying to make is that Thomas would not listen to anyone as he could trust no one after the barbaric way he had been judged and executed. He was also falsely accused of robbery and a third murder. Thomas's mind was conditioned into thoughts that he would end up in the fires of hell that had been preached to him before he died. That is why Mary took on the important task of carrying out Thomas's rescue to send him towards the light. The real reason that she succeeded where others had failed was the fact that she spoke to him with a mother's love, telling him that she, Penry and Irene had truly forgiven him. Moreover, that he was still their son and that, no matter what he had done, they still loved him very much. This paved the way to help the guardians to prepare to come and collect him. When they arrived to take Thomas away it was very emotional indeed. When he asked Mary why she, Penry and Irene had found it in their hearts to forgive him, she replied that it was because they loved and supported him. This was the crucial time when the barriers came down and the guardians had arrived to take him away. Thomas cried out, 'Oh, Momma!' It was at that point all over.

I am pleased to say that recently Thomas has sent a lovely message through to Mary via myself, expressing his thanks for rescuing him and that he is now happy and progressing quite nicely. A mother's love is very potent indeed; I would say it could move mountains – look what it did for Thomas.

When I requested that Mary, Penry and Irene should visit the places where we the Wyndhams had lived, I felt a surge of excitement. After visiting the tavern they were quiet and in deep thought and yet excitement welled up inside them. We were travelling back in time to the 17th century, trying to imagine what it really looked like. They visited all the places of which we Wyndhams were once a part. I myself, although I visited with them in my spiritual body, felt rather strange, because Weaverham had changed so much since I and my family had lived there. All the beautiful open fields had almost disappeared, the tavern played strange music and was noisy with people's laughter and the clinking of glasses. There were strange engines going at great speed, which I have learned you call motor cars.

I remarked to all three that I much preferred the quietness that I knew from my time. When the horse and coach would go at a nice steady pace and I could at least hear the birds singing, wave and bid good morning to my neighbours.

People in your era do not seem to find time to breathe. Everyone seems to be constantly in a great hurry and the noise from your machine engines must I fear contribute to people going quite deaf in time.

Although our lives were quite barbaric and hard in my time, I am afraid that I would willingly not exchange that life for the way that you good people live today among noise and seeing those lovely fields diminish to make way for progress in the modern world.

Dear Charles was a wonderful friend to the Wyndham family as well as myself. We often tried to console him in his moments of loneliness, isolation, and sadness, which affected him because of those he could not trust around him. Our friendship was very strong indeed and we honoured him. We loved him for the person that he was; we were not in awe of him because he was the king. Our friendship has continued into the next world.

I look back on all the atrocities I witnessed in Weaverham. It makes me feel sad but not bitter for I learned a great deal through going through all those different experiences. Charles I, I am sure, feels the same way as I do; it was part of our learning. We both strive from the place where we now dwell, for we have very important work to do from this side of life. Even those who took Charles's life, including Oliver Cromwell and those puritan soldiers who took away my earthly life, all have had to progress, learn and advance on this side, and they have all felt ashamed and saddened when it has been pointed out to them the wrongs and the atrocities they carried out on their fellow human beings.

For progress is open to all. Everything that is achieved on this side of life is not done for gain, except for love and advancement of one's spirit. One earthly life is likened to a vast schoolroom; we are given free will to choose which way we wish to go. Everyone is brought into this world with a guiding influence, or whatever you wish to call it, a guardian angel. Mary is often asked the question by people of the reason why, when we leave this earthly body and pass to this side of life, how on earth do those in charge on the other side, as people wish to call it, know about everything good and bad that we have done while dwelling on the earth plane. The answer my friends is that the guardian angel I mentioned to you, or guiding influence, knows you as a person better than you know yourself. Therefore there is no fire and brimstone, you judge yourself for the person that you really are and some people feel pleased while others feel ashamed when shown their actions when they occupied their earthly bodies.

However, once people accept where they are and it is explained to them that they can put things right, then they feel so much happier. In fact, some people are shocked when they are shown how selfish they were when they dwelt on the earth plane. During this lifetime they were totally oblivious to how selfish and disruptive they really were to their fellow man. Such love and understanding is given from our side but we also have to adhere to rules and regulations just like you have on your side of life. Even your beloved pets reside with you on this side, until it is time for them to move on and evolve themselves. Animals also have different temperaments and characters and we have an animal kingdom where all animals live together in total harmony for they also have had to learn.

I was well pleased to hear from the guardians who are appointed to dear Thomas, that my brother is progressing nicely. Although Thomas is working, very hard to come to terms with what he did, he still feels overwhelming sadness at his crimes. By eventually helping others when he finally progresses, then and only then will he be set free in his own mind. Thomas has declared to me that it is an uphill struggle to come to terms with his conscience and when I am allowed to visit him I am a constant reminder of the time in September of the year 1658 when he took the lives of my wife Margaret and daughter Anna in a fit of temper because he could not claim the title of lord of the manor.

I do have regrets about Thomas. If only he had sat down and thought about the consequences of his actions, things would have been so very different for him and my own family. We are all responsible for our actions. Even thoughts that are released from people are very important indeed. Always keep your thoughts pure; never send vindictive thoughts out, all your thoughts are registered. Even if you have a sick relative or pet you can send loving thoughts towards them, wishing them to recover from that sickness. Thought is powerful. Loving and kind thoughts also help to make you a much better person; it helps to keep you in harmony with the vast universe that permeates around you.

Chapter 14

The Spiritual Schoolroom

People with prominent titles like Charles I and Oliver Cromwell, once they make their transition to the other side, at once lose their earthly titles, for here you are known by what you achieved in your earthly life. Even your own royal family, when they too pass over to our side of life, will instantly become ordinary people. There are no labels attached to you to say how famous you were when you occupied your earthly body. Many famous people when they come over here are so relieved that they do not have the pressure on them any more that they had to endure while living in an earthly body. They have complete freedom to do as they choose providing they where a decent person in your world.

The spirit world is also inhabited by those souls who, when they resided on the earth plane, had people waiting on them hand and foot. They thought that they were so powerful that people should live in fear of them constantly. I am afraid that they are in for a shock when they come to reside here, for they have to learn that everyone who resides in these realms are on an equal footing; no soul is better than another. Everything in these realms is achieved through pure love; those people who take it upon themselves not to listen and still maintain this arrogance are placed with other selfish people who led debauched and selfish lives similar to them until, one day, they ultimately learn that progress is the only way forward and the only way to escape from the dark conditions that they created for themselves.

We are all part of God and no man should think that he could dictate and try forcibly to own another person. Everyone on your earth plane is placed there to learn and to grow and progress together. It is, as I have mentioned before, likened to being in a schoolroom and, if one realises that we are here to grow spiritually together, then the schooling can be most pleasant. However, it is only by making mistakes that we learn. Everyone is given free will to choose on which pathway they wish to embark. Some roads are quite rocky and dark but always remember you do have a guiding influence to help you. You are never alone on that road, even if you think you are.

I have just been talking about our titles but, of course, once you pass over to the spirit world you no longer need these titles for these are man made. They may be necessary while we inhabit the earth plane but, once you make your transition to this side whether you are king, queen, prince, lord or whatever, you no longer need these titles, for no one is recognised by how important they were or from whence they came. The all important factor here is to help each other with great love and understanding. To love one's fellow man is far more priceless than a magnificent jewel in a crown. I think now you may understand my meaning. The love I now have is something far more pure and intense than I ever experienced while on the earth plane. Nothing is done here for gain – only for love of the purest kind.

It is wrong for any man to take another man's life. I have learned from this side of life, that for anyone to retaliate against someone who tried to harm him, does not solve the problem. When I stepped in to save the life of the king when Angus Larchwood conspired to kill him, I did wield my weapon but did not use it to kill him. I was in a very strong position to do so but, fortunately, I let my higher self take over, which is one's own spiritual self. I view things far differently from where I now reside. I am so pleased and happy that I did not take this man's life, for life is not ours to take in the first place. It was not my wish to see Angus Larchwood in a dirty rat-infested dungeon to die of tuberculosis. Because of the seriousness of his offence, the crown incarcerated him in this place and I was powerless to stop it because the king had already granted him his life. I do not feel hate for this man, only sorrow because of what he had brought upon himself, but I am glad in my heart that I took it upon myself to visit him.

Wars do not solve anything; there are no winners, Your world has a great deal to learn on this subject. We in our world have people residing here, who engaged in battle against each other. Now they realise how silly and fruitless it all really was and now they actually work together for the betterment of humanity. They try to impinge on the thoughts of those in your world that are planning to engage in warfare. It is always the poor unfortunate bystanders who end up suffering because of their leaders taking them into battle of which, most times, these poor people do not want to be part in the first place.

When wars are made – normally out of greed – I do wish you could see how hard we in the spirit world have to work in helping souls over who are in a state of shock because of leaving their physical bodies so quickly, through being shot or blown up when not expecting this to happen. We must think before we act. Mary's father was drowned in November 1939 because he lost his footing on a darkened ship. The blackout was enforced as war had been declared on 3rd September. So even in this instance, a valuable life was lost and Mary lost her father in the physical sense but, thankfully, her father now communicates with her from the spirit world.

Weaverham is steeped in history, in particular the tavern that was used for prosecutions and hangings which left many negative vibrations behind, built up layer on layer. All the sadness attached to the place came naturally from the sad vibrations left in the building. Mary, Penry and Irene, visiting the tavern a few times and speaking to those souls there still in limbo, assured them they could go towards the light. This lifted all the negativity from within, so that the place is now light, airy, and most pleasant to visit. Even from the comfort of their own homes, they would send those loving and healing vibrations towards the tavern and this added to the power to release anyone still trapped between the two worlds.

Some souls can be trapped between the two worlds for centuries. As in the case of Thomas, everyone in that position can be and is eventually helped over to the other side. They are often pulled to strong memories of the place were they dwelt; of course, the guiding influence talks to them and explains that they have passed on. Some souls do not want to believe this because of purely feeling so alive, and they find it hard to believe that they are no longer on the earth plane.

This is where patience is required and the guiding influences leave these souls a little longer; no pressure is put upon them whatsoever. In Thomas's case, he took over three hundred years to realise, that he had wasted valuable time staying in limbo. I have already mentioned that this rescue of Thomas only took place because he felt the tremendous feeling of love and compassion from his mother. This unlocked the door of his inner prison within the confines of his own mind and all ended happily, I am pleased to say.

Not one single person is left to flounder for many of them are afraid to let go of earthly ties and this is quite understandable. There are specially trained people in the spirit world, whose job is solely to help these poor souls, and I must say they do a wonderful job. We have caring and compassionate workers here who send out so much love and they are totally dedicated to helping those souls who feel alone and lost, caught between the two worlds, We are indeed fortunate to have such lovely people amongst us.

It is extraordinary that, during times of great sadness, people seem to find time for each other. I find it a great pity that this does not occur during happy times in people's lives. For example the villagers in Weaverham managed to muster so much strength, love and compassion for their fellow man that there were many acts of extreme bravery.

Intense sorrow seems to unite people in such a wonderful way enabling them to create a deeper understanding of each other's needs. During the war that started between Britain and Germany in 1939, there where many acts of bravery and kindness to each other; people buried there differences and pulled together. Why does it take a war or a major catastrophe for people to find love and compassion within themselves? These feelings of love should come naturally.

Chapter 15

The Weaverham Papers

There were two books written about Weaverham and the Wyndham family. The first one was written in 1864 telling of the connection between Charles I and the Wyndhams. Unfortunately, this book was destroyed in the war when the building it was stored in was bombed. The second book was compiled and written on the history of the village by Mr Barkman but never published; he had a distinguished looking beard and moustache. He settled in the village in 1899 and, in 1902 after considerable research, with the help of the local people, he began writing the book. Although this book was never published, he wrote some informative papers on the history of the village which travellers bought when passing through. Mr Barkman knew nothing of the link with King Charles and found it fascinating to sit and listen to the locals. He loved the history connected to Weaverham and, of course, he fell in love with the tavern, although this historic place has been used for many different things since then. It was used as a butcher's shop in your time, then it was a bookshop and newspaper shop. Now it is a wine bar but always a very interesting building indeed.

It is quite wonderful I think that you in your time can shoot across the skies in flying machines that you call aeroplanes, arriving at your destination the same day. I find it quite fascinating that your ships go at great speed and the cars you have in your time travel very fast indeed.

However, as I have mentioned before ,I would still prefer my trusty steed but I do realise that you in your time need these machines. In my time, it could take weeks or many months by ship to certain destinations and it was so hazardous because of severe storms at sea and, of course, pirates and other war-faring vessels. Yes indeed times have changed but I myself prefer a much slower pace.

People from other foreign lands heard about what had taken place in the village of Weaverham and travelled over by ship in the 1800s to view the place for themselves. Such was the history of the place that people came and they for ever asked questions. Some of these people liked what they saw so much they stayed.

I do feel so strange each time I re-visit with Mary, Irene and Penry; as I have said before, it looks vastly different to me now and to see so many of your machines on your roads. In my time, we only had what you would call dirt tracks and our horses went at a good steady pace. These sturdy lovely animals never let you down and I have very fond memories of my faithful steeds.

Marten and his wife Eliza have earned themselves a most beautiful place in the realms of light. He and his wife now teach young children the correct way to live a spiritual life through love and kindness. The little ones on the other side love them both and simply cannot wait to join up with them, and to rejoice in the pure love they receive from them both.

As for those people who carried out the terrible murders in Weaverham, like Moembah and the puritan soldiers, they have spent all this time since the 17th century trying to work out the crimes they committed against humanity, trying desperately to come to terms with what they did, with their conscience tormenting them. It will be a long hard road for them but it is the only way for them to learn one important factor, they have to learn that every human being is part of God, even themselves, that no one can destroy anything that is created by God. It is an insult to the greater intelligence to take a person's life by force. There is a plan set into motion for you and you can upset this plan by being arrogant and selfish.

Progress is open to all and one would be foolish not to attempt to put things right. You must endeavour to move forward. We on this side of life understand that you most certainly are going to make mistakes and we do allow for this. If you knowingly set out to hurt a fellow human being, then you only hurt yourself by taking many steps backwards. The road to progress will become that much longer; we give you a choice, the rest is up to yourself. Seek out the higher self.

Children in my time were most innocent and untarnished; they led such wretched lives in the fight to survive. The children in your time have a much better education and better standard of living compared with the little ones in our time. We in the realms of light have our work cut out. It pains and saddens me to receive young people over to our side who have foolishly taken drugs to such an extent that they have cut short their earthly life. If only you could see all these lovely young people just embarking on their earthly life, coming over to the spirit realms. After some time when they become accustomed to where they are, they feel such sadness at the realisation that they no longer live in their physical bodies, and shock sets in.

People in your world need to be responsible and know that this dreadful problem with your young ones, and adults, is getting dangerously out of hand. We send warnings from our side to your world but I am afraid no one wants to listen.

Even your earth is suffering when thousands of trees are needlessly chopped down, starving the earth of oxygen. God created a perfect universe and he expects you to try to replace all you have been taking; man cannot keep taking. The North American Indian race used what they thought was needed for they loved the land, which they called Mother Earth. If they had to kill an animal for food, they would pray over it to ask forgiveness for taking its life. Therefore, you should also have the same respect, not only for the animal but also for yourselves and your actions, for your own body is a temple.

We on our side of life do honour many souls who eventually come over to this side; particularly those who serve their fellow man unselfishly like Marten and his wife who gave those little children the chance to live and be loved once more.

To serve is most wonderful without thought for oneself, to reach this side of life after dedicating one's life in serving mankind brings about the most wonderful rewards. Not in money form, for we have no need of it here, but in the spiritual jewels that one may have acquired in your life. When you arrive here you are known by the beautiful vibrant spiritual colours that permeate around you. This is all the recognition you will need. All we ask of you is to stop, think and try to change your thoughts; to think deeply on what you are doing to your world before it is to late.

From where I now reside, I have been shown on film man's great achievements travelling to the moon and back, with giant rockets also travelling into space. Now there is talk of man planning to live on space stations.

Vast amounts of money are being spent, not only on these rockets but also on research; some travellers into space have even sacrificed their lives. You have not even solved your problems on earth, and yet people are setting their sights on reaching space.

Millions of people are dying from poverty; your rain forests are suffering; people are dying of this terrible disease of aids mostly brought about by man. I think the research should start on your earth plane, money and resources should be given to those poor souls who are suffering. Is it not also important to help ittle children in the third world countries who suffer from malnutrition and contaminated water? Before we reach for the skies, we must put things right round and about us first and foremost.

In practically every country on your earth plane there is war or threats of war. That is why it is so terribly important to put right first this earth plane of yours. Each country must try harder to live in peace with others. You all gather your scientists together from each country to try to conquer the skies. If only different nations could come together like this to solve the problems of earth and bring about peace and unity. Then maybe, one day, when man has solved the problems of the earth plane, he can be ready to conquer space because all will be well on earth.

Shelaise Petifer, the lady who helped some of the orphaned children of Weaverham, is carrying out a wonderful job in our world as a very fine healer. She loved children and her work still carries on from this side. Even in your time small children and older ones come over traumatised and we on this side of life prepare healing couches for these little ones to receive loving attention and healing from ladies like Shelaise. They receive beautiful healing rays in lovely soft colours. A child may have suffered a long illness and known nothing but pain during a hospital stay while on the earth plane. They no longer have this pain in the body, but the memory of that child still carries that realistic pain it had endured during that illness.

The lovely soft healing rays soothe the child's mind and help the little one to adjust to its new surroundings; so many are helped in this way. Shelaise and other bands of healers work hard and steadfastly with so much love and compassion to nurse these children. We have so many on this side who work solely with children because they are experienced and dedicated. In addition, many of these wonderful helpers have had jobs as nuns, nurses and teachers on your side so they are also good at counselling the children. However, the main ingredient to have for this job is of course a great love of children.

So you see if you loved children, animals, or just your fellow human beings there is a good opportunity for you to work with whatever makes you content and happy on this side.

I mentioned to Mary that the music now played on your side of life is so very loud and quite tuneless. We feel the tremendous vibrations as we draw near to the earth plane. If only you could hear the music over here – sweet mellow sounds that would melt your heart and lift your spirits. If you are truly interested in music, then the opportunities will be open to you and we have beautiful concert halls. Each note that is played sends out its own vibration of colour and our orchestras play to perfection. If you love to sing there is no one here to criticise you; only love and support is given and you also can reach perfection. I still love to play my flute, hopefully a little better than when I dwelt in Weaverham!

Great writers and poets, great men and women of your time reside here, and anything they did not manage to achieve on the earth plane is most certainly achieved here in these beautiful realms. Even people who loved to tend to flowers and trees, learn to understand the workings of Mother Nature in its finest of detail. Wonderful talented artists from your time still hold exhibitions of their work here for people to view. May I say that they are breathtaking, because the artist has all the time in the world to perfect these glorious works of art. Never have I smelt such a beautiful perfume in all of my life than in the flowers that grow here and the flower colours on the earth plane are dull in comparison.

Charles I, as I have mentioned, was a fine artist in his own right; he was so happy and thrilled to meet up with some of your great artists. In our time, they would require a great deal of money, to be taught even the basics of learning to paint. Everyone is born into your world with some sort of talent or gift. Some people may be slow academically but they may shine at playing the piano. being able to hold people's attention with whatever they may be playing at that time. You may fail at one thing only to shine at doing something else. The king worried when he was in your world about learning different languages, for it was important that he should learn, he being king. When you reside here you can even learn different languages, not that it matters, for there is no need to speak in these realms for everything is done by thought process. Even on your earth plane, your pet, the dog or cat, instantly picks up your thoughts and knows what you are thinking. People who reside here learn different languages because they did not have the opportunity to learn when they were in the physical body. I have had to learn modern day English because when I arrived I spoke only in old English. If I had not taken it upon myself to learn, then dear Mary would not be able to understand me. Moreover, this could have led to difficulties in the writing of this book. Where I reside I still refer to a pen as my quill and I do laugh so at some of the modern sayings that Mary speaks. She has to explain to me what they mean, otherwise I am perplexed.

Chapter 16

Annie

There was in Weaverham, at around 1900, a lady called Annie, an excellent medium of that time. She was quite large in stature but she was a true and steady worker for the world of spirit. In those days, the ladies would have to be most careful, as the Witchcraft Act had not been repealed. Messages from mediums were held behind closed doors. For a lady to consult a medium was almost unheard of but the few for whom Annie had already given sittings had begun to trust her because of the astounding evidence she provided. She brought comfort and peace of mind where it was most needed; men feared her but they also felt intrigued with her. She needed great courage to carry out this valuable work in her day.

Her family arrived in Weaverham with Annie when she was a babe in arms; only fourteen months old, from the place she liked to refer to as the Emerald Isle, Ireland, The family settled quite happily in Weaverham. Her mediumship was invaluable, for many of the ladies simply did not know which way to turn. The gentlemen of course would not dare to present themselves to Annie but I doubt anyway if this lady would have taken the chance to accommodate the men with sittings. She also possessed the gift of poetry and she would often sit on her quieter days and write the most beautiful inspirational words.

There were many fine mediums such as Annie in those days but they had to be most careful of the authorities. People would scoff at these people not realising that they were born with this wonderful gift to enable them to help people. If the medium was genuine then she brought untold comfort to some poor souls. You now have many mediums in your world. We from our side of life like to remind people who work for the spirit world that they must be honourable and truthful at all times because, if they are not, then they are only fooling themselves. It is a great honour to work for the realms of light but it is a very great responsibility to us, your fellow man and to yourself. You must only draw to you that which is pure and good. We on this side do not require workers with egos.

You may ask why we require booking a sitting with a medium, what purpose do they serve. They are the intermediaries between the two worlds. The reason being that, if you should lose a relative through death, you may spend days, months or even years grieving for that loved one, thinking that they ended up like grains of sand and they exist no more. This is not so and it is at this important stage that the medium does a valuable job. If the medium is spiritual and genuine then he or she will have the capability of bringing that loved one close to you. You must remember that your loved one must be ready for communication, for they to have to learn to communicate to your world and sometimes they come through showing great emotion and love to you. It helps to sow the seed within yourself and if you receive a wonderful and genuine communication from that person you had thought had ceased to exist, then you sit down and start to think deeply and this awakens a spark within you. There is no death, my friends. Jean, Mary's mother in this life, fretted and pined for many years because Mary had lost her father through drowning. Mary, even as a small child, tried to comfort her mother and tried to reassure her that her father was alive, because, as a child, Mary sensed her father was around her and her mother. However, she was so overcome with grief that she caused Mary's father who resided in the spirit world to feel so sad that he was prevented from drawing too close, because of the barriers that Mary's mother had put up in her own subconscious and the vibrations around her.

It is important, when through physical death you lose a relative, that after the initial shock you endeavour to send loving thoughts to that person because by carrying this out you are helping that loved one to adjust into their new life on this side. By sending those loving thoughts, you help them to awaken much quicker. Moreover, the time then can be shortened and in no time, after valuable instruction from this side of life, they are ready to communicate with you, if they so desire. The love link that you had with that person can never be broken. I have said this before, that I love my parents. Mary, Penry and daughter Irene, after a span of over three hundred years. Does that not tell you something of the potency of true love.

If everyone in your world would get together in concentrated thoughts of love, peace, healing and compassion, what a huge difference it would make. If only you could view the darkness of the earth plane from where I reside, we also on this side feel all the sad vibration emanating from your world, sadness pain and suffering.

For we on this side of life have to lower our vibrations in order to penetrate your physical matter that is a great deal denser in substance, may I say.

The darkness that we see could be turned into pure beautiful light, if only people who reside on the earth plane would take the time to send those pure and beautiful thoughts into the world. Sending healing thoughts to every country in your world to penetrate and reach every dark crevice would bring astounding results, to say the least. People in your world do not realise the power of thought which can move mountains. Every thought that you release must be a loving thought. Always think before you release a bad thought because there is such a thing as cause and effect. Whatever thought you release, good or bad, comes around full circle back to you. Even dear Thomas has had to learn this valuable lesson, of how potent our thoughts can be.

I spoke of gifted artists in our world; a wonderful psychic artist called John Brett created the picture you see of me. Many people on your earth plane are mediumistic and are able to see the subject that they are about to paint. You may wish for one of your relatives to sit to have a portrait painted. However, remember that when a person passes to this side of life, they take all their habits with them. Their personality does not change. Therefore, they may feel too shy to come forward to sit in front of one of these gifted psychic artists so you may have to be patient for quite a while. This gentleman is a very fine artist indeed and I may say that he is very well respected on our side of life, for we appreciate these people who bring alive that loved one that you thought you had lost.

The great halls of learning that I myself attend on this side of life are vast and they are never ending. Mary has written the truth through my guiding influence, every minute thing that has happened on your earth plane is stored here for all to see and only the truth is written here. History is recorded as it really happened, not what the historians have written about. Nothing has been added; only the truth is recorded here. For the spirit world records everything that happens on your earth plane the very second it is taking place. My family and I lived through the horrors of the 17th century and on arriving on this side of life, there was no need to feel upset and aggrieved at what had taken place, trying to explain what we had gone through. The time that I had lived through had already been recorded for posterity in the realms of light.

That is why it is so important for your world to change. God created a beautiful world for you to nurture and to take care of. Is it asking too much? Everywhere that the great teacher walked (I am referring to Jesus now) there is nothing but bloodshed and fear and this makes me feel so sad. When you make your transition to this side of life, you may visit the great auditorium to sit with hundreds of other people to listen to Jesus when it is his turn to give a lecture. He explains the reasons why he came to teach people. Also there are other great speakers that you can listen to which is quite fascinating. I do wish you could see the beautiful colours that they carry around them, for, the higher evolved a person is, the colours become more vibrant and they seem to have movement.

When a person offers up a prayer, you may often wonder if the prayer is answered. It all depends if that prayer comes from one's heart and soul and for a good reason. The guardians of light who dwell in the higher realms receive your prayers by thought.

Even if they think the prayer should be answered, they cannot answer it straight away for they have to wait for certain conditions to happen in your life so that they can bring about an answer to the prayer. However, they can intervene if they feel that it is a dangerous situation, which needs immediate attention.

When a person is on their deathbed and they may not have led a very good life, it is of no use suddenly praying for forgiveness. For that person must wait to go over and be given the chance to put things right, that is if they truly mean to change.

Shelley one of our most famous of poets has contributed this inspirational poem that he wrote himself in the world of spirit. I feel this poem also carries a warning to mankind that people on the earth plane must start to consider and respect this perfect world that God originally bestowed upon us with such love. I feel that as the writer of this book I am very privileged indeed that Shelley should have written this beautiful poem quoted here.

A poem written by Percy Bysshe Shelley

Upon the souls of man

Upon the souls of man
with mind like a window with insight find.
Yet think he not clear and conscience does find
through his pittance of lost emotions does raise his own distraint.
For strife is real enough to encase him in learning
be that on his own accord.
A mark of respect he does wither a forgotten pose of reject for he should
 awaken and account himself before his own bereft.
Countless are the gifts man bestowed
and comfort he can withhold.
From watching angels who abide by life's unfold.
No man may seek solace where man has brought pain
he will not find his place in heaven and shall not ever gain.
Unless he can equate himself to be in goodness and array
And become less of himself to pride and show mercy to others.
For it is not that God in purpose felt to trust all souls
seeking compassion and making true life's entrust.
But by his own self indulge in oblivious mistrust.
See clearer vision of a world ending and waste.
But it is blessed not deprived of a mere haste
of humanity unscathed.
Should man now not carry
justice for life's future we are afraid

This transcript was given by Arun, a Templeate Knight, on 4th February, 1999.

This young gentleman offered this contribution to the book:

'My name is Arun, a Templeate Knight.

'It is with great pleasure that I bring this to you. I appeared in my time in great tournaments; we were filled with great enthusiasm. I served the young Harold. I bring ye all that I can bring for the men in your world do raise the sword with each other. Not knowing of the great consequences we only had mock battles to honour ourselves or our king. Why man does take up the sword in hand, I fear he also does not know that there will be no achievement and he will gain nothing. It is inevitable that thyself and many others like me in our world who now are preparing those in your world who do bring battle upon themselves and men who do not wish to allow this to happen. We are acting upon our wishes to bring peace to your world.

'I, Arun, speak for the spirit world: let not man put asunder his people. I am bade to come forth by my guardians and I am deeply moved with emotion carried by such conditions which devastate your world.

'I bid you farewell and God bless. – Arun.'

Second Transcript from Arun

Arun began by explaining to us how he became a Templeate Knight, an order of knighthood formed by Sir Gordon Balsfriars from 1402 until 1438. Sir Gordon was Scottish and the order was based on Harold from the eleventh century; Arun was a descendant of Harold.

Arun said that the name Templeate meant that which is sacred. Moreover the Templeate knights were strong believers in king and country and did not surrender to those who would ravage the land. Sir Gordon Balsfriars taught Arun of his strong links with Denmark and Harold, for the code of the knights was based on a very old order which has carried through to our time.

'I, Arun, became a knight Templeate at the age of sixteen years, the title being bestowed on me by Sir Gordon Balsfriars on 18th August 1429. I passed to the spirit realms in 1436.'

A transcript from Rebecca, 4th February, 1999.

'I was called Rebecca but my father in biblical times wished to call me Naomi. In our time we did not call someone after another; I am now called Rebecca.

'I come to communicate with you great gifts, which God has created in your world – the God force.

'The power that succeeds is everything that man can progress towards, that he himself has accomplished to bring himself towards the time now which is what you have called your millennium. For you in your world now, there are many that already have an awareness of great change. The spirit realms have those who work to ensure that you, in your world, are aware of such facts that we will establish and bring to enlighten the souls of man. It is our duty to lead those who, by their birth, have come to the earth plane to carry out that work which is so necessary, so that brothers and sisters, in its spiritual aspect which you all are, can begin to be a true part of each other. It is the children, those who are born to mothers now, that must be taught about a spiritual self, so that the future can be a direct meaning of life. I, Rebecca, am so troubled by your children; I feel their emotions in your world.'

Nostradamus came through with this transcript to help the world on the 4th February 1999.

'I, Nostradamus, come forth as I did write of many conditions which, as I predicted, have come correct in your world. I do now say there is more to come. For now I can let you be aware, and I have been asked by those guardians in the world of spirit to give presence to you and to state that my final prediction can be taken into account unless man will serve those positive vibrations that are very much alive. For I have been granted to bring this information to this world, as what I knew is what I know now. Please, mankind, I beg of you – you must be prepared for the consequences that will fall on the heads of man. He ignores all that he has been given to unlock that which has been buried within his karma; I must go now. These words are awakenings for man to see for himself. – Nostradamus.'

This transcript was given by John the Baptist on the 4th February, 1999.

'For I, John, performed baptism for the people.

'I was the gentleman you would call John. It was in my heart I had great faith for I truly did serve and walk with Jesus. This is how his name has been derived. For you in your world he was a great medium and healer and did help those around him. I myself carried out healing to the sick as, in that time I am speaking of, we had a great illness which we ourselves learned was worsened through lack of knowledge. We soon learned that the healing gift was bestowed upon us to use. There are many ways that mankind can combine all feelings that are eminent within himself. There is much goodness that man carries and this goodness can be put to such good use. For he is able to make peace where there is no peace, to bring harmony where there is upset. He can bring healing to the sick if he looks within the deepest part of his soul. He will only begin to be aware of such inner gifts that are born unto him. He can suppress those conditions with learning as this must come from man himself.

'Many blessings from one who still likes to think of himself as a humble servant,

'John the Baptist.'

My thoughts

I do hope by reading this book you will have been given a deep insight into what took place in Weaverham in the 17th century. You can be sure that love never dies. Recently I had a spell of ill health and as I lay in my bed, I sent my thoughts out to dear Patrick and Thomas. In an instant they both arrived by my bedside and they lovingly stroked my head and they in turn immediately sent their thoughts out to the realms of light requesting healing for their dear mother. I receive so much love from my two wonderful sons who both still dwell on the other side.

At least I was most fortunate to have been born a lady of the manor and I lived in relative comfort apart from the dreadful atrocities which took place at that time. You may ask why I came back into this life of worry darkness and strife the answer is simple you must have balance in the 17th century. I lived a comfortable existence. But in this life I have had to experience suffering of every description; it is only by suffering that one can realise what other fellow human beings are going through. I have been brought back not only to help people but to also write the truth about what happened to Charles I, Patrick and Thomas.

I feel very humble also to know that King Charles I was a very close friend of mine. Patrick tells me of intimate conversations he had with the king. Patrick sat for many hours with him trying to allay his fears. I now feel very privileged to receive communication from Charles from where he now resides in the realms of light – and what a lovely gentleman he is. I thank all my friends who reside on the other side for they are my true friends. I thank them for giving me the opportunity to give something back to them and also offering the truth to our world.

There is no death it is only an extension from this life for better things to

come. It gives us all a chance to grow spiritually and to serve our fellow human beings God bless all whom have contributed to this book.
Mary.

This transcript was given by Malo on 14th January 1999.

Malo is a much evolved soul who holds a very important position in the realms of light. He met and admired Jesus for Malo himself was born in Bethlehem. Moreover, he has promised to write through Mary in her next book, to try to bring enlightenment to this very unhappy world.

'I was very privileged to meet with Jesus when I resided in Bethlehem. He was a great man but he was also frowned upon at times. He did have a very difficult task before him. The light he did contain within himself was the pure power of love for his fellow man. I did truly admire and understand this very kind and giving man. I myself was a quiet man in my own way; I also wrote my own text when I walked the earth plane. It was a very poor time for everyone for we were all extremely poor.

'Your world must change. We, the guardians from the other side of life, are well aware of what is taking place in your world. During the millennium, great changes will take place. We have come forth to help this world with great love and understanding. I, Malo, cannot reveal to you any more about these changes but know that we are here. We at one time have had to walk the same rocky road that you are now treading. I Malo am now highly evolved in the realms of light; we shall make you aware of the many aspects of your soul.

Malo

This is a second transcript given by Malo on 4th February 1999.

There are those in your world who seek compassion, yet they do not have this for it is up to those who are spiritually aware to give this where it is needed. There are many conditions in your world which must be enlightened according to spiritual law, if man puts in order that which is necessary. That is putting negative energy into positive energy, then, encircling his whole being with light, he can only make your world a stronger force of survival. He must look within his own spirit and find that which is goodness itself, to enable your world to grow and to have safety for what is to come. The future, as you will know it, will be guided by the influences you create. This must be an ultimate awareness of knowing what man can do to create the balance, which is so needed. We are the watching angels, yet we can only help by protecting mankind for as much as it is possible. We in our world know that this is significant and must be

99

nurtured, for the progress of all souls that are in your world and those who will yet come. Your future is in the balance. Please do not create difficulties which will not serve mankind or each other, as it is only positive conditions which stem from your spiritual self that transform you into the light.

'God's blessings be with all mankind – Malo.'

Explanation of the Six Helpers:

These six helpers all explain in their own ways, saying exactly the same things – that men must change their own thoughts to one another and how they act towards one another. Greed and the acquisition of material gain must cease and love towards their fellow men must be the major force in everything that they so desire.

Also Malo, the guardian, is preparing people for great changes during the millennium. If men react to those messages, they can avoid disaster.

Malo, the Guardian of Light